PRAISE FOR

NEXT MISSION

"I loved *Next Mission*! Part lighthearted memoir, part insider's guide to diplomacy, and part cautionary tale of the dangers of allowing politics to stand in the way of sound diplomatic work, this is a very engaging and revealing work. I hope people come away from *Next Mission* with a new appreciation for the intricacies and nuances of US foreign relations and, just maybe, a new appreciation for our relationship with France and the French people."

> —SUSAN EISENHOWER, CEO, President and Chairman of the Board, The Eisenhower Group

"Rick Steinke pulls back the curtain on diplomacy in France! Read what Ian Fleming could only pretend to know about Paris!"

> —DENNIS MANSFIELD, Coach, Speaker and Author of *Beautiful Nate, Finding Malone* and *To Trust in What We Cannot See*

"Colonel Rick Steinke recounts his fascinating professional and personal journey as the Defense Attaché to France during the most strained period with our oldest ally since Charles de Gaulle expelled US forces in 1966. From politics, international relations and military affairs to backcountry Alpine skiing and overseas family life, *Next Mission* is a 'can't put down page-turner' that should be made required reading for military officers, diplomats and anyone else stationed abroad."

> —MICHAEL SCHMITT, Charles H. Stockton Professor, U.S. Naval War College and Francis Lieber Distinguished Scholar, U.S. Military Academy at West Point

"What a wonderful Franco-American journey of discovery! Superbly told and most entertaining!"

—COLONEL DEB LEWIS, (USA, RET), Best Selling Author, Local Business Mavericks

"A frank, marvelously descriptive, and heart-warming rendition of what it means to be a Military Attaché and an Army Family in a foreign country. Colonel Rick Steinke's (Ret) wonderful tale of his time in France as Defense and Army Attaché during a time of troubled American-French relations is a wonderful tribute to the professionalism, resilience, and character of our military and foreign service members and their families."

—MAJOR GENERAL GORDON B. "SKIP" DAVIS, (USA, RET), Deputy Assistant Secretary General for Defense Investment, North Atlantic Treaty Organization (NATO)

"Rick led what was widely considered the most highly functioning defense and security attaché team in Europe during a time of intense US-France bilateral relations. This book shows why personal leadership counts."

—PETER N. LENGYEL, President and CEO, Safran USA (former defense security cooperation officer, U.S. Embassy Paris)

"This is a remarkably candid view 'behind the scenes' of a military family serving in Paris on an important mission for America. Rick Steinke presents a fascinating storyline that's easy to follow, shows the uncommon and even dangerous challenges that a military officer on attaché duties has to overcome, and adds incredible historical details along the way. It reads like a novel—I could not put it down! Should be required reading for officers young and old."

—LT GENERAL MARK O. SCHISSLER, USAF (RET), Former NATODeputy Chairman of the Military Committee and Harvard National Security Fellow

"This extraordinary book is by an officer and a gentleman who passionately served his country while also respecting France. Colonel Rick Steinke personifies the meaning of duty. At their core, his responsibilities were every bit as demanding as they were dynamic and exciting."

—MAJOR GENERAL VINCENT DESPORTES, (FRENCH ARMY, RET), Former Commandant, French War College and author, Entrer en Stratégie and Deciding in the Dark

"A remarkable account and reminder of some exceptional moments in Paris. One such moment occurred on a dark winter evening, while en route by train and bus to the French Alps. As guests of the French Army, I met and sat nearby a gentleman with whom I quickly discovered shared common interests and approaches to mine. During our French alpine week, after taking a humble approach to our skiing abilities, we were promoted to ski with our highly skillful—and somewhat surprised—Austrian, Swiss and Nordic attaché colleagues. This marked the beginning of two years of close cooperation with the US Defense Attaché to France, Colonel Rick Steinke."

—VICE ADMIRAL IOANNIS G. PAVLOPOULOS, (GREEK NAVY, RET), Honorary Commander in Chief of the Hellenic Fleet and former Greek Naval Attaché to France

"The mystery of military diplomacy is simplified in this masterful chronical of the geopolitical challenges surrounding the ascension of Colonel Rick Steinke as the US Defense Attaché to France. Rick's flair as a superb story teller keeps the reader entranced as he provides insights into real people facing real issues while achieving real results. His education, foreign language skills and 24 years of Army leadership experiences prepared him well for his pinnacle military assignment. A must read for anyone interested in learning how diplomacy really works and how to lead in a volatile environment."

—COLONEL HERMAN BULLS, (USAR, RET), Vice-President, Jones Lang Lasalle Americas

"*Next Mission* is an enthralling read. Its fluid narrative superbly depicts the delicate context in which a Defense Attachè operates, while at the same time catapulting the reader into several situations which vividly represent the 'journey' that a Defense Attachè goes through—the emotions, the concerns, the planning, and the strategies. *Next Mission* exposes them all. This book is also a near-perfect reflection of my experience as a Defense Attachè at the Italian Embassy in Skopje. A must-read for anyone looking to take on the very demanding Defense Attachè role!"

—MAJOR GENERAL LUIGI FRANCAVILLA, (ITALIAN ARMY, RET), Former Commander, Italian Army Aviation Forces

"Through his exceptional memoir Colonel (Ret) Rick Steinke has gone further than anyone in asserting the critical role played by military advisors in US and international diplomacy. He has also successfully stomped out the much-exaggerated notion that an attaché's work mainly involves 'protocol, alcohol and cholesterol'. Outstanding . . . well worth a read!"

"My own posting alignment with Colonel Steinke's tenure in Paris provided an extremely rewarding opportunity to develop both a close working relationship with Rick, and by extension a warm personal relationship with him and his family. I was able to experience firsthand his outstanding professionalism as he met the challenges and lived through the highlights recounted in *Next Mission*. He captures succinctly, with trademark passion and enthusiasm, the broad spectrum of professional and domestic issues that inevitably present in such a key international relations appointment—always striving to achieve the best possible outcome for his country. Tout à fait well done!"

"In *Next Mission*, Rick Steinke shows how bridges in international diplomacy need to be built long before they may need to be crossed. Fostering international partnerships is truly the linchpin to 'one team, one fight', keeping the United States and our allies safe from the many evils in today's world."

Next Mission
US Defense Attache to France:

A Memoir from the Days of
"Punish France, Ignore Germany,
Forgive Russia"

by Colonel Ralph R. "Rick" Steinke
(US Army Retired)

Published by

 köehlerbooks™

210 60th Street
Virginia Beach, VA 23451
800–435–4811
www.koehlerbooks.com

NEXT MISSION

U.S. DEFENSE ATTACHÉ TO FRANCE

**A MEMOIR FROM THE DAYS OF
"PUNISH FRANCE, IGNORE GERMANY,
FORGIVE RUSSIA"**

**COLONEL RALPH R. "RICK" STEINKE,
(US ARMY, RET)**

VIRGINIA BEACH
CAPE CHARLES

DEDICATION

To Susan, whom I asked to travel the world—and serve my country—with me more than thirty years ago. I was blessed beyond measure when you said "yes." In France, you made my mission *our* mission, and I could not have asked for a better friend, confidant, teammate, and mother to Erika and Maria!

To Erika and Maria, for the indescribably wonderful God-given blessings that you are, for faithfully adapting to our many moves and homes, and for becoming the amazing young women you have become.

To Gonzalo, Sofia, Isabela and Elena, wonderful blessings all and the newest additions to "Team Steinwald," for the love and hope of a bright future you have brought to our family.

To my mother, Erika Sofie Steinke, one of the most generous, enthusiastic, faithful, optimistic and life-embracing people I know, and without whose personal example of how to live, I would not be half the man I am today.

To my courageous, funny, and tough father, Sergeant First Class (US Army, deceased) Harvey Ferdinand Steinke, who taught me how to throw a pretty good curveball, how to catch a mess of perch (along with my grandfather, Alfred Steinke), and so much more, and whose example of military service set me on my own path of service to country.

To my brother, Glenn Christian "Chris" Steinke, for always being in my corner, and for being a caring and generous uncle to Erika, Maria, Sofia, and Isabela.

To the *other* "1 percent": all of my fellow Americans—and especially the families who support them—who have sworn to serve and sacrifice in defending the Constitution of the United States of America. My eternal and humble gratitude to those who sacrificed all, as well as those who bear the scars—emotional, mental, or physical—of their sacrifices.

DISCLAIMERS

The views expressed in this publication are those of the author and do not necessarily reflect the official policy or position of the US Department of Defense, its components, or the US government.

All events and conversations depicted herein were reconstructed to the best of the author's recollection.

CONTENTS

FOREWORD

FEW BOOKS HAVE BEEN WRITTEN about military attaché duties. A character portraying a military attaché may turn up in a spy novel, an international political thriller, or more often than not, a motion picture placed in a military setting. Those portrayals are often audience-accepted caricatures rather than factual reflections and accurate composites of the real deal world of attaché duty. This memoir adds real-world color, based on actual experiences, to the intentional grays presented in those venues. Travel with Colonel Rick Steinke and his family as they arrive in Paris and the author describes taking on a new military mission during arguably the most difficult period of U.S-France relations in the post-World War II period.

- Get the inside view of the nuanced diplomatic conflicts that occur serving in a major US embassy. See what it is like and experience the challenges of representing the US Department of Defense and Armed Forces to a country that the United States government has suggested it will "punish" due to disagreements over the Iraq War in 2003.

- Visit the meticulously maintained and sacred American Battle Monument Commission cemeteries in Europe and see what it's like to plan, organize, and execute the Sixtieth Anniversary of D-Day ceremonies, including a visit by the President of the United States.

- Experience parachuting into the Normandy countryside near St. Maire-Eglise, made famous in World War II by American paratroopers' liberation of that Normandy town.

- Get a glimpse of US Congressional delegations visiting the US embassy in Paris and discover the importance of personal relationships in high-stakes diplomatic relations.

- Read about particular experiences such as attending English-speaking churches in Paris and skiing in the Valle Blanche, a high-altitude and physically challenging glacier with ever-changing seen and unseen deep crevasses in the shadow of Western Europe's highest mountain, Mont Blanc.

In a sense, become Colonel Steinke's personal "attaché" as you read this story—walk with him through events that no international spy novelist could capture, no international fiction writer could develop, and no motion picture producer could film.

Nothing beats reality. Nothing.

Dennis Mansfield
Author, Coach, and Speaker
http://www.DennisMansfield.com
https://www.facebook.com/DennisMansfieldAuthor

CHAPTER 1

DIPLOMATIC DRIVE-BY

A DIPLOMATIC RECEPTION THAT FIRST September provided an unpleasant surprise. A sort of diplomatic "drive-by" occurred on Chile's National Day and the anniversary of my first month in Paris. At just past 7:00 p.m., after presenting my French diplomatic ID card and our reception invitation with handwritten names on it to a gendarme officer outside, my wife, Susan, and I breezed through the electronic screening and entered the Chilean Embassy reception.

We then passed through the receiving line, which included the Chilean Ambassador and his wife. We also said hello to the Chilean defense attaché, Colonel Domingo Navarette, and his wife, Haddy, before moving into the chattering crowd of uniformed and business-suited international attachés and diplomats. Susan, a fluent Spanish speaker, soon saw an attaché spouse she recognized, and they quickly struck up a conversation.

As I stepped up to one of the self-serve buffet tables to reach for some finger food, a slightly accented male voice behind me blared in English, "So, the United States is going to just preemptively attack anyone whenever it wants, just because it *thinks* it *might* be threatened?"

Turning around, I was surprised to see Colonel Yokiaki Ishi, the Japanese defense attaché to France. I had never met him before but had seen his photo in the *Annual Foreign Attachés Accredited to Paris* guide, as well as at a previous event in Paris. He was looking straight at me. I was also aware that a lot of nearby eyes and ears were fixed on both of us, some pretending not to be interested but clearly listening. Feeling quite gobsmacked, I realized he was expecting an answer.

As I processed what was happening, I thankfully recalled that the United States had just published its new National Security Strategy the previous day. While I had made a mental note to read it, I had not yet reviewed the full document. I did, however, remember reading an internet-published story about the most controversial and prominent aspect of the strategy: that the United States' preserved the right to *preemptively* attack an enemy—a state or non-state actor—if it determined that enemy posed a direct threat to US national security. In other words, the US reserved the right to attack another state or non-state actor without having been physically attacked first.

I sensed both displeasure and an ironic sincerity in Colonel Ishi's voice. *Was he* sent *to deliver this question—and perhaps thinly veiled message—to me . . . or was he just expressing a personal opinion?* I pondered. Given his direct approach, I thought it had to be the former.

"Well, what would you expect after the 9/11 attacks?" I asked the colonel.

Not knowing what else to say, I left it at that. It would not be the last time I answered such an in-your-face question with a question of my own during my tour in Paris. Upon hearing my response, Colonel Ishi turned around and walked away without another word.

Is this *how diplomacy is supposed to work?* I asked myself. *With somebody walking up behind me and blurting out a question, a question obviously meant for others to hear to as well?*

Released September 17, 2002, barely a year since the attacks on the Twin Towers and the Pentagon, the 2002 National Security Strategy (NSS) presented the Bush administration's first comprehensive justification for a new, aggressive, *unprecedented* American approach to national security. Calling for *preemptive* action against hostile states and terror groups, it stated that the US "will not hesitate to act alone, if necessary, to exercise our right of self-defense by acting preemptively."

CHAPTER 2

WELCOME TO PARIS

AS OUR BOEING 777 LANDED at Charles De Gaulle airport northeast of Paris at just after 8 a.m. on August 19th, 2002, following almost eight hours of overnight flying from Washington Dulles Airport, a day that had been filled with much personal and family anticipation had finally arrived. As an Army officer who had alternatively served in operational assignments "with troops" and in "Foreign Area Officer (FAO)" international assignments, I was about to begin a new FAO mission: US Army Attaché to France. Little did I know that in less than six months, I would serve in the significantly more responsible and higher-profile position of US defense attaché (DATT) and senior defense representative to France.

The next four years arguably marked the worst political relations between the United States and France since World War II. During this period, it would be my mission to represent the Secretary of Defense, Chairman of the Joint Chiefs of Staff, United States Armed Forces, and people to the French Minister of Defense, French Chief of Defense (CHOD), French Armed Forces and people. I would also serve as the senior US military advisor to the US Ambassador to France.

Additionally, it would be my duty to keep senior US policymakers apprised of French and European regional political-military activities and affairs. Supporting US military theater security cooperation and assistance programs in France, which included over thirty US liaison officers or students attending French military schools, from the French military academies to the *Ecole De Guerre*, would also be part of my job description.

Landing on that hazy August morning, I did not know the adversarial US-France political climate about to develop. I did not know one of my primary missions would also be to ensure that US-French military-to-military relations did not suffer significant or even irreparable damage. I would have to do my best to ensure that political acrimony did not endanger US-French combined military operations, and more importantly, the lives of US—and French—soldiers.

A result of markedly divergent, emotional, and very public US-French political approaches on what to do about Iraq, a belligerent Saddam Hussein, and those elusive weapons of mass destruction, US-France political relations would be strained in the months ahead. As the Senior US Defense Representative to France, I would find myself at the crossroads of that strain.

As my wife, Susan, my daughters, Erika and Maria, aged ten and four respectively, and I made our way off the plane and on to a large, standing-room bus, we were quite excited. The excitement was mixed, however, with a bit of nervous anticipation, especially from Erika. As a "military brat," Erika once again had to leave her friends behind. This was her fifth move in the first decade of her life. This time it was her friends from southern Yorktown, Virginia, whom she had to say goodbye to. To soothe their concerns of what might be ahead in this new and strange land called France, Susan and I promised (okay, bribed) the girls that we would take them to Euro Disney, located on the eastern outskirts of Paris, at the first opportunity.

After about a five-minute bus ride, we offloaded and entered the main terminal through some of those automatic glass and steel doors found in terminals around the world. We then followed the crowd through more doors and narrow corridors. Finally, after what seemed like walking through a maze, we reached Passport Control. Here we entered the "Non-EU (European Union)" line. We eventually had our newly issued black diplomatic passports stamped before trudging on to the large baggage claim hall, where we discovered that, fortunately, all our bags had made the journey from Virginia. On we walked, pushing our loaded baggage carts past the French customs officials who were surveying the arriving passengers.

After we walked through the largest—and final—automatic sliding door, a new world greeted us, abuzz with spoken French and a smattering of Arabic and English. In front of us was a sea of signs with personal names, corporations, tours, etc., printed or hand-written on them by the awaiting taxi and limousine drivers who held them. Also evident was a culturally mixed crowd of awaiting relatives, friends, and colleagues—and searching eyes, many looking towards or past us as we pushed and pulled our luggage clear of the big doors.

My eyes, in turn, searched the awaiting crowd for my "sponsor," Army Major Eric Peterson. For transient US servicemen and women in the United States or overseas, sponsors play a key role in smoothing the transition and trauma of distant and frequent military moves to new posts and organizations. Eric and his wife Jenny had taken over from my earlier sponsor and predecessor, Colonel Andrew Manuele, who had departed earlier that summer for his next assignment.

Both Andy and Eric did an excellent job answering the many questions presented by Susan and me . . . but mostly by Susan: *What housing is available? What about the schools? Should we send our kids to a French school or an international one? What about medical facilities? How about grocery shopping? What does a quart of milk or dozen eggs cost in Paris? Is the subway safe? Is the* **city** *safe? How far are the nearest US military facilities? Are the French waiters as snobby as portrayed in some movies?* The list went on.

The person I saw next recognized me at about the same instant I recognized him. My reaction to his presence was somewhere between bewilderment, humility, and pleasant surprise. It was US Air Force Major General (Select) Felix Dupré. He approached us wearing casual civilian clothes. A military uniform would not have been appropriate here, certainly not from a security perspective. Next to him was his always energetic and enthusiastic wife, Lin.

General Dupré and I had met earlier in the summer in Washington D.C., on more than one occasion and had gotten along quite well from the start. However, I certainly did not expect him, an air force general officer, to be meeting me at the airport.

I had served twice previously as a US Army *foreign area officer*. The first time was as an exchange and plans, operations and training officer ("S-3") with an Italian "Alpini" (Alpine Infantry) battalion. This roughly 700-man battalion served as Italy's contribution to the North Atlantic Treaty Organization's (NATO) Mobile Force (Land), composed of about 5,000 men and women from seven NATO nations, including the United States. The Mobile Force's mission was to go into harm's way, as the first NATO response, to any potential or ongoing Soviet attack against any NATO country in Europe. I would later serve on a shortened nineteen-month tour as a liaison officer from the US Army Training and Doctrine Command to the Italian Army Staff in Rome. I expected this foreign embassy assignment to be different, but not so different as to have an Air Force general meeting my family and me at the airport.

"Rick, Susan, girls . . . welcome to Paris!" General Dupré exclaimed, adding in a lower voice, "Rick, we're going to do great things together."

"How was your flight?" said Lin.

"It was great, and thanks to both of you for being here," I responded.

"Great to see you both again!" added Susan.

The Duprés' presence at the airport was all the more surprising since they had only arrived in Paris some ten days before we did. They had their hands full with their own move-in activities and challenges.

Yet, somehow, they managed to find time to give my family and me a warm welcome to Paris at the very moment we officially stepped onto French "soil." That was one of the many examples that I would observe over the next few months of Dupré's caring and committed leadership.

Standing about five feet, nine inches, with a solid athletic build and slightly graying black hair, Dupré was instantly likable, with calm confidence and an easy sense of humor. He would also turn out to be a heck of a lot of fun to serve with. A former US Air Force F-15 Eagle fighter pilot, he had commanded airmen at every level from flight through wing command. Just before coming to Paris, he had also been selected for promotion to major general and a second star while serving on the Supreme Headquarters, Allied Powers Europe (SHAPE) staff in Mons, Belgium.

General Joseph W. Ralston was a US Air Force four-star general who commanded all NATO forces (from sixteen countries at the time) as well as United States European Command. He was Supreme Allied Commander, Europe. And he had supported Dupré, his then-executive officer, to be the next US defense attaché (commonly called DATT) and senior US defense representative to France. A two-year tour of duty (most US military attaché tours are for three years), the defense attaché position in Paris rotated among the Army, Navy, and Air Force. In the summer of 2002, it was the Air Force's turn to fill the slot.

US Secretary of Defense Donald Rumsfeld approved Dupré for the position. Replacing a flag officer (a naval officer above the rank of captain) who spoke little French, Dupré was the perfect choice to serve at US Embassy Paris, one of three US embassy locations—Beijing, Moscow, and Paris—in 2002 that had a general or flag officer as US Defense Attaché.

After some quick small talk, we met one of the Defense Attaché Office (DAO) drivers, Pascal Illand, who helped with our bags and led us to two curbside vehicles, where Dupré's driver Thierry Fleuet was also standing by. My family and I, with all of our luggage finally in the back of the Chrysler minivan, piled in through its open side doors. The Duprés then got in the back of the US embassy-provided Volvo sedan, parked just in front of us and driven by Thierry, and returned to Paris. Two minutes later, our fully loaded van departed for our new home on *rue Prony*, in Paris's seventeenth *Arrondissement* (district).

CHAPTER 3

MOVING IN

AS WE MADE OUR WAY southwest to Paris down highway A1, I didn't think the traffic was all that heavy, especially for a Paris-bound Monday morning. It was busy but flowing, certainly not as heavy as when Susan and I visited for a few days the previous April. Entering Paris from the north and continuing from block to block in a southern and then westerly direction, I was even more struck by the *very* light traffic.

I had taken a semester of French as a 45-year-old student (with some basic French self-study already under my belt) at William and Mary College, and then several weeks of night school in Washington D.C. I put all that to the test now with my first French of the day, asking Pascal, *"Pascal, Le traffic . . . Pourquoi est-il si léger?"*

I then waited for a moment, and he fortunately came right back in French with, "It's the vacation period. Everybody is on vacation."

Of course, almost everyone *was* on vacation. Much like in neighboring Italy and, as I would later learn, other countries in Europe, from August 15 through the 31st, give or take a couple of days on either end, the vast majority of Parisians were out of Paris and at the beaches, in the mountains, or traveling abroad. The summer exodus actually begins the day after Bastille Day, July 14, and continues apace until mid-August, when it shifts into a higher gear. It's tourists who mostly occupy Paris during this late-August period.

Pulling up to our six-story granite apartment building on rue de Prony, I was impressed by the massive wooden door at the main entrance. One could only access it by punching in a numerical code or electronically and remotely unlocking it from inside the building. Pascal had the code, which he entered for us. The door opened to a stone alcove leading to an open courtyard. A few steps to our left, we beheld an archway leading to a flight of stairs and an elevator that would take us to our upper floor apartment and new home. On the right, we later learned, was the small apartment that was home to the building concierge and his family.

The elevator accommodated no more than three cozy adults at a time. Susan, Erika, and Maria took it and ascended to our apartment. I decided to take the stairs. Reaching our third-floor apartment with the ladies already anxiously awaiting, I inserted the nickel-plated skeleton key Pascal had given me. I turned the audible tumblers of the heavy, dark green metal doors, and the door popped open.

We then entered a hallway that led to adjoining living and dining rooms on the street side, as well as a modestly but sufficiently appointed kitchen facing the inner courtyard. The ceilings, perhaps twelve feet high, made the roughly 2,000-square-feet, three-bedroom apartment feel even larger than it was. A nice touch, common to these apartments built in the late 1800s, was the (nonworking) fireplace and large mirror above it in the living room.

Painted off-white throughout (which Susan's eye for warm colors and talented painting hands would soon change), it was not ostentatious. The adjoining living and dining rooms did, however, make the apartment well-suited for the representational entertainment that Susan and I would do for the next almost four years. Guests would include the French Army chief of staff, French and international flag officers and diplomats, and many senior members of the large international, diplomatic military attaché community present in Paris.

After discovering her bedroom toward the back of the three-bedroom apartment, Erika came back to the kitchen and opened the refrigerator.

"Hey, Mom, Dad, look! There is food in the fridge!"

Thanks to Lieutenant Colonel Bill Cosby, my senior assistant Army Attaché, Erika had discovered enough staple foods—milk, eggs, cheese, bread, butter, salami, beer, and other items—to keep us from starving until we discovered the nearby local bakeries and supermarkets. In the kitchen cupboards, we also found a few other necessities, such as laundry soap, dish soap, and a bag of those "goldfish" that Maria was partial to. In the closets, there were even a few clothes hangers.

And then, on a kitchen counter, I saw a note. My experienced eye could see it was on the unmistakable stationery of a US Air Force general, with white stars on a blue background. I read the *handwritten* letter out loud to everyone gathered in the kitchen:

Dear Rick, Susan, and Family,

WELCOME to Paris! It is great to have you here, and we're looking forward to very good times ahead. Hope your "settling in" experience is smooth and that your move is uneventful. Some numbers if you need them:

Cell 06-20868749
Home 01-42655922
Again—welcome! See you soon.

Felix and Lin

This very thoughtful and positive message was yet another gesture that helped make Susan and me confident that we were off to a rewarding assignment, no matter the challenges.

Thanks to our sponsors' diligence before our arrival, the apartment was also sparingly but sufficiently furnished with some modest, temporary, but entirely useful US Embassy-provided furniture, probably dating to the 1960s.

"I can't believe how well this place has been prepared for us," I commented to Susan.

It would take another two weeks or so for our furniture and household goods to be delivered, some of it from long-term storage in Hampton, Virginia. However, the embassy-provided furniture began to make this otherwise sterile apartment feel like home.

After Pascal and Thierry finished helping us get our luggage upstairs and bid us *"Au revoir, mon colonel et Madame, à demain,"* we decided to unpack for no more than half an hour before going out to investigate the local neighborhood. We consulted the neighborhood fold-out map our sponsors had mailed to us. My first official appearance at the US Embassy would wait until the next day.

Our unpacking almost complete, we headed down the broad and creaky wooden staircase and out the door to rue Prony, our new street and neighborhood in the seventeenth *Arrondissement.* After we hit the inside buzzer to let ourselves out through the big door, we stepped over the door's lower frame and onto the sidewalk. Our eyes were quickly drawn to the left, where there was a traffic circle and metro stop sign called Pereire.

Walking toward the traffic circle named Place du Maréchal Juin, we noticed a small park with grass, a few trees, a couple of park benches, and some flower beds inside the traffic circle. This would provide the closest place to walk our soon-to-arrive, Virginia-native golden retriever, Lucky.

As we made a left turn on the sidewalk, clockwise to the traffic circle and flow of traffic, what would become our local café, Café Royal Pereire, came into view. At just after 11:00 a.m., a bit late for an early morning *café crème* but too early for lunch, it had only a handful of customers among its fifty or so seats. Continuing, we were about to cross rue de Courcelles when we looked to our left and down the street. Susan spied some red neon letters that said *Monoprix*. We then remembered from our brief trip to Paris the previous April that Monoprix was a French supermarket chain. That would be our first stop.

Soon exiting the Monoprix with a few sandwiches, groceries, and, of course, a baguette and bottle of red wine, we turned right and headed to the next corner of rue de Courcelles and rue Pierre Demours, where the words *pâtissière* and *boulanger* came into view on the building at the corner, now to our immediate right. We had found a local French bakery! But the sign on the grated security gate took some air out of our enthusiasm. It would be closed until September 4.

"Even Paris's famous baguette makers are on vacation!" said Susan, who had studied French with me during the previous nine months.

From there we decided to press on to *Avenue de Wagram*. In Paris, an "avenue" is wider than a "rue," and often lined with trees. A "boulevard" is even wider and often multi-lane. Avenue de Wagram was named, like other streets and places in Paris, after one of Napoleon's victories or one of his most prominent field marshals. In this case, it was named after the decisive French victory over the Austrians on the Marchfeld plain, northeast of Vienna, in 1809. From the corner of rue Courcelles and Avenue de Wagram (more accurately, due to the trees lining the street, from the median of Wagram) we saw one of our first memorable sights of France: our first ground view of the distant Arch of the Triumph, of which we could make out only the top portion.

At that point, we determined to walk down Avenue de Wagram in the direction away from the Arc de Triomphe and toward rue de Prony, in effect beginning to circle back to our apartment. As we walked past the Elyfleur flower shop, I remembered what a retired colonel and former US Army Attaché to France had told me about that place:

"If you're ever in the doghouse, it's a great place to stop on the way home, even late at night, as they maintain quite long opening hours."

Try as I might over almost four years not to have to follow that colonel's advice, it indeed turned out to be invaluable counsel.

On our side of Avenue de Wagram, at the corner with rue Gounod, was another place that got our attention: *Lenôtre*. It was as if the purveyors of Lenôtre knew every culinary delight—and weakness—known to man: macaroons, *foie gras*, smoked salmon, lobster tail, chocolate truffles, ice cream, caviar, *pâté*, and the list went on. It was a gourmet heaven. However, the prices reflected the exceptional quality, and while we would venture there a couple of times our first year, we only returned for very special occasions.

As we arrived at the corner of rue Prony and Avenue de Wagram, we turned around and were amazed at how clearly we could still see the Arch of the Triumph. Then, before turning left and walking down rue Prony and back to our apartment, we looked to the right, in the southeasterly direction down rue Prony. At the end of the street, we could make out a columned edifice with a dark dome, surrounded by green vegetation. Checking our map, we saw that the building was on the edge of a verdant area called Parc Monceau.

While I would spend long days in the US Embassy and officially around Paris and beyond, the girls would visit Parc Monceau before I would, much like many other places in Paris. Susan had a good plan for showing the girls many of the Paris sights. Her bloom-where-you-are-planted attitude as an Army wife would serve us well in Paris, as it had in several other places—California, Indiana, Massachusetts, Missouri, Oklahoma, Virginia, Germany, and Italy—during our fifteen years of marriage.

Heading back to our apartment building, we entered through the large street-side doors to meet a mid-forties, relatively tall man of slightly dark complexion with black hair and brown eyes. He introduced himself as Monsieur Cousin, our building concierge. I found his French accent a challenge to understand. I was relieved, however, to see he understood my introductions of the girls to him.

Using part French and a little sign language, Monsieur Cousin indicated the door that led to his ground-floor apartment. It was adjacent to the street entry, from which he could monitor the occupants of the apartment building as they were coming and going, as well as visitors and anybody not known to him. As the girls then headed up to our apartment, he showed me where the underground parking spot was, as well as the location of our designated basement storage area, deep in an old basement. The space had a dirt floor, and when the timed hallway light went out, it went pitch-black. Stephen King would have had a field day writing about it. Besides being useful for storing a few excess household items, it became an excellent place for storing wine.

Finally arriving back upstairs myself, I was happy to see Susan and her little helper Erika making a light lunch. Maria, in the meantime, had lain down on the corner bench in our kitchen and passed out. By the late afternoon, with the overnight flight from Dulles now a distant memory, we were all exhausted. Susan and I knew the fastest way to adjust our sleep patterns to our new time zone would be to go to sleep as close to our normal bedtime as possible, which, back in Virginia, had been about 10:00 or 10:30 p.m. for us and earlier for the kids. But after almost thirty hours, we had to force ourselves to stay awake until close to our normal bedtime. Otherwise, the jet lag would have wreaked havoc with our sleep schedules over the next few days.

So Susan and I took an early evening walk down to *Parc Monceau*, which turned out to be a lovely expanse of green with a mix of coniferous and deciduous trees, as well as running trails and flora. We returned to the apartment by 7:00 p.m. We had asked the girls what the first thing that they wanted to do in Paris was, and Erika had responded, "See the Eiffel Tower, of course!" At 8:30 p.m., we went to the taxi stand, and by 9:00, we had our first family picture in front of the brightly sparkling Eiffel Tower.

CHAPTER 4

PARIS EMBASSY: DAY ONE

HAVING WOKEN UP AT 4:00 A.M. DUE to the jet lag, I was thankful to have brought some reading material along. This included Samuel Huntington's *Clash of Civilizations and Remaking of the World Order*, which I was rereading. While I did not agree with everything in his book, I was fortunate to have met Professor Huntington at Harvard's Belfer Center in the fall of 1998. In lieu of Army War College attendance, I was at the nearby Harvard Kennedy School (who said the Army didn't have a sense of humor?) as a National Security Studies Fellow. In 1998, Professor Huntington was still esteemed as one of America's foremost experts on civil-military relations, having written the seminal work *The Soldier and the State* in the late 1950s.

At about 8:00 a.m., wearing a sport coat and tie, I looked over our wrought iron balcony and down at the street to see if Pascal had pulled up. As I did, I noticed a black car . . . perhaps a Mercedes Benz? As I stood there for a few seconds admiring the pristine paint job, out of the car stepped Pascal.

"Pascal?" I half-mumbled to myself.

Looking up to our balcony, Pascal, who had apparently heard me, offered a subdued *"Bonjour, mon colonel!"* just loud enough for me to hear but not so loud as to awaken the few Parisians who might still be sleeping in this otherwise quiet block of Paris.

"*Bonjour, Pascal*," I answered. "*J'arriverai dans trois minutes!*"

At this point, I realized Erika was standing beside me on the balcony, while Susan and Maria were coming through the dining room to the balcony to see what the commotion was about. Looking down at the black car, Erika, who would turn eleven in two months, asked, "Dad, are we *rich* now?" Even at her young age she knew that automobile down below was quite different from our Volkswagen Jetta Wagon.

"No, sweetie, that car doesn't belong to us. It belongs to the embassy," I answered. To Erika, "emassy bembassy" the car just as well might have been from the moon, but I had made my point that it was not ours.

Susan simply said, "Not bad."

After we kissed and said goodbye, I headed for the front door, where I had pre-positioned my briefcase with all of my military orders and documents. Grabbing the briefcase, I exited the apartment, then bounded down the staircase and out the door of the apartment building. Pascal opened the right rear and curbside door for me, but I insisted on sitting next to him, up front. When I grabbed the door handle, the door's weight immediately conveyed that this was no ordinary Mercedes. It was armored. Closing the door took an extra bit of "oomph," which I embarrassingly underestimated on my first try.

I later learned that General Dupré had sent "the DAO armored car"—which was mainly intended for *his* or a visiting VIP's use—to come get me. It would be seven months or so before I would ride in this car again, and under completely different circumstances. It was normally only used when the local threat conditions were high, or during an official Paris visit from a high-ranking US officer or government official, which normally meant at least a four-star flag officer or higher civilian official.

This vehicle meant our DAO had also received authorization to travel in the vehicle to or from a residence. This authorization was not automatically granted, certainly not for all US defense attaché posts. It was often based on local threat conditions. Less than a year after the 9-11 attacks, security threats to Americans still loomed large.

Paris was by no stretch of the imagination Baghdad or Kabul (where I would later serve). But US military attachés had been murdered at or near their posts around the world, including in Athens, East Germany, Manila, and right here in Paris. On January 18, 1982, the assistant army attaché and decorated Vietnam veteran, Lieutenant Colonel Charles R. Ray, was murdered from behind and at point-blank range by a Lebanese militant affiliated with the Lebanese Armed Revolutionary Faction. Lieutenant Colonel Ray had parked his car about 100 meters from his apartment and was headed there in the morning when the Lebanese assailant walked up behind him and pulled the trigger.

I would learn from a US embassy security officer that a US Embassy Paris deputy chief of mission ("DCM," second to the ambassador and the *chargé d'affaires,* in charge of the embassy, in his absence) almost met a similar fate. While walking on the sidewalk, the DCM noticed a suspicious individual and soon realized the man was armed. He immediately took evasive action, eluding his intended assassin's pistol-fired bullets by ducking between parked cars. This saved his life. The intended assassin soon fled.

Some six years after Lieutenant Colonel Ray was assassinated, a German diplomat, Siegfried Wielsputz, met a similar fate in Paris. Felled by a gunman from the Kurdish National Liberation Front in January 1988, Wielsputz became the eighth international diplomat killed in Paris in a ten-year period.

From a security perspective, there were habits my family and I would have to break. For example, growing up, I was taught to answer the phone with "Steinke residence." In Big Rapids, Michigan, that was a perfectly normal and courteous way to answer the phone. Not so for a uniformed US military officer in Paris. Answering with your name could assure any nefarious caller that he had the right telephone number and that you were home, and later, if you did not answer, that you were likely not at home. The simple French "hallo" would have to do.

Another security precaution involved the wearing of jewelry. Other than a wedding band or a watch (if that counts), I was never a big fan of jewelry. However, wearing a college (or high school) class ring was a *no-go*. Except for some Liberian or Caribbean countries' military officers, whom I once observed wearing similar rings, very few other countries on the planet that I'm aware of have adopted this tradition. If you are wearing a school class ring, chances are about ninety-eight percent that you are an American. When riding a subway and putting your hand, about shoulder high, on one of those chrome poles to stabilize yourself during the ride, it might be seen by a half dozen or so nearby strangers, from perhaps as many countries, all crammed next to you. In a Paris subway, or many other places outside of the US, for that matter, it's probably better *not* to make it evident that "here stands an American."

On this, my first day traveling to the embassy from my new home, the drive turned out deceptively easy. It would take us under fifteen minutes to connect from *rue Prony* to *Boulevard Malesherbes* and then drive southeast from there to *rue Royale* and the *Place de la Concorde* before we reached the US Embassy, on *2 Avenue Gabriel*. Two weeks later, with the Parisians having returned to Paris for *la rentrée*—the mass "return to work" from vacation—that fifteen-minute, two-mile trip would have taken twice as long, and during Paris's worst traffic jams, easily an hour or more.

As we approached the embassy, I could see concrete security pillars about a meter high positioned outside the embassy fence. These were intended as obstacles, located to establish a "standoff distance" for any vehicle-borne suicide bomber. There were also four very visible French *gendarme* officers, positioned after the 9/11 attacks, not at the request of the US Embassy but at the insistence of the French government. Two gendarmes were standing on the sidewalk about forty meters in front of the external Marine guard post. A third, roving guard was on the corner of *rue Gabriel* and *Place de la Concorde*, and the fourth was standing on the sidewalk near *rue de Boissy d'Anglais*, running between the main embassy chancery building and the famous hotel to heads of state and Hollywood stars, the *Hôtel de Crillon*. Other gendarmes could also be seen in the general local area.

Instead of driving me through the embassy gates and into the embassy subterranean garage, Pascal let me out of the car curbside. I stepped out and immediately showed an approaching gendarme my diplomatic passport, along with my military ID card. After his *"Bonjour, mon colonel"* and my *"Bonjour, monsieur"* response, I was immediately met by a man in his mid-thirties. Approximately five feet, eight inches and with a stout build, he said, "Good morning, sir. I'm Sergeant First Class Ralph Weld. Welcome to the US Embassy!"

"Thanks much, Sergeant Weld. Great to be here!" I replied.

"Follow me, sir," said Weld as he led me to the Marine guard post, about thirty yards from the embassy front doors. The embassy's security fence extended from both sides of the guard post. As I opened the heavily armored guard post door, I noted its weight: Weld gave me an assist as I finished pulling it open.

The Marine corporal manning the guard post took my black diplomatic passport and military ID card, and exchanged the two documents for a temporary visitor's badge. The visitor's badge would allow me access within the embassy until I received a permanent embassy badge with photo ID.

"Make sure this badge is easily visible at all times, sir," the corporal firmly stated.

At this point Sergeant First Class Weld led me out of the guard post and slightly downslope to the sidewalk, which led to the front doors of the main embassy chancery. To my right, in the small, well-kept grassy area, I saw a life-size statue of Benjamin Franklin. He was seated on a park bench, leaning slightly forward on his cane as if to support himself.

Having been dispatched to Paris not long after signing the Declaration of Independence, Mr. Franklin, then holding the title of commissioner, can best be described as the first ambassador to France of the American colonies, then newly self-declared as independent. His presence in Paris put it on the map as America's first diplomatic mission. Being in his seventies (and a favorite of the French high-society ladies), Franklin was instrumental in negotiating the 1783 Treaty of Paris, which successfully concluded America's Revolutionary War. He ended up spending nine years in Paris, not returning to America until 1785.

As I walked up the short steps to the main embassy doors, there was another Marine guard post just inside the building and to the right of the doors. This guard post was also protected by slightly smoked, heavy blast-proof glass. I made sure the Marine standing on the other side of it could clearly see my badge. As soon as she did, she hit the buzzer inside, tripping the heavy locks open and allowing Weld and me to pull open the doors.

Once inside, I beheld a large atrium with a sparkling marble floor and very high ceilings, perhaps twenty-five feet. Little did I know, right behind me there were two large—approximately ten by four feet—full-standing oil portraits of two French heroes of the American revolution: Marie-Joseph Paul Yves Roch Gilbert du Motier, more famously known as the "Marquis de Lafayette," and Jean-Baptiste Donatien de Vimeur, comte de Rochambeau, more commonly known to Americans as the "the Comte Rochambeau" or General Rochambeau. I would not see their portraits, like I did most days later, until I exited the building later in the day.

Suddenly, to my left, I heard: "Colonel Steinke, good morning!" It was my sponsor, Major Eric Peterson, who added, "Sorry I did not meet you at the airport yesterday! I wanted to, but General Dupré waved me off."

"Eric, I get it, no problem! Thanks for all you've done in getting my family and me squared away to this point."

"My pleasure. Let's head up the DAO spaces."

I followed Peterson as he led me to an elevator and then the third floor, and on to a back-corner hall, where we then descended three steps to a robust, dark oak wooden door with cypher locks. As we reached the door, Peterson pointed out the wooden shelving to my left, purpose-built for cell phone storage, and said, "Please leave your cell phone here, sir."

I complied, picking a small cubicle in the bottom right so I wouldn't mistakenly grab one of the other cellphones already there.

Right before punching in the cypher code and going through the doors, Peterson introduced me to two French interpreters whose joint office was just outside the "classified" area of the DAO. Both ladies were in their thirties.

"Sir, this is Nicole Guillou and Laurence Clary," he said. "They are our excellent interpreters."

"Hi, I'm Rick, pleased to meet you," I said.

"It's a pleasure to meet you, sir," said Nicole, and Laurence followed with, "Good to have you here, *mon colonel.*"

Relieved that they did not test my French, I followed Peterson through the door and into what would be my main working area for almost the next four years.

After we cleared the door, Major Peterson said, "Sir, let's go to your office so you can drop your bag. Then, I'll introduce you to the rest of the team, at least those folks that are not on leave today."

My new office, just big enough for the fairly large wooden desk and Army-issue brown vinyl visitor's chair, was actually fairly close to the entrance. Therefore, I did not need to go far into the roughly 2,500-square-feet area. These DAO spaces accommodated what, at the time, was one of the largest US Defense Attaché offices in the world, as well as one of the largest office sections of US Embassy Paris.

Before my first day was complete, I would meet Louis "Deak" Childress, the US naval attaché (also "ALUSNA," a holdover acronym from the title "American Legation United States Navy Attaché"), a Navy captain, former F-4 Phantom and A-6 Intruder pilot, and affable bear of a man from southwestern Virginia. I would meet his assistant, Navy Commander Patrick Braker; the Marine Corps Attaché, a logistics officer, Lieutenant Colonel William Holdorf; an Air Force F-16 pilot and Rhodes Scholar, Colonel Jeffrey Jackson; and my other Army assistant, an Army lieutenant colonel, Lieutenant Colonel William "Bill" Cosby.

In all, including Lieutenant Colonel Mike Kelley and Major Chris Moffett, assistant Air Force attaches; and an Army major, Major Jeffrey Kulmayer, who served as a liaison to the French Joint Staff, there were eleven commissioned officers assigned to the US Defense Attaché Office—USDAO, Paris. There were also other military officers on the embassy country team, such as the Chief, Office of Defense Cooperation, US Army Colonel Dorothea Cypher-Erickson, and her staff, who came under the overall leadership umbrella of the Defense Attaché but whose direct chain of command led back to US European Command in Stuttgart, Germany.

After meeting the attachés, I got to meet the people who kept the entire office on track, and without whom we would be dead in the water: the noncommissioned officers, the sergeants, led by US Army Chief Warrant Officer Four Patrick Derby. Chief Derby had been around the block as an attaché operations officer, knowing all of the administrative ins and outs of the support side of attaché duty. He also served on the Embassy Housing Board, which allocated, as fairly as possible, the embassy's housing pool to incoming US Embassy Paris employees and their families. This was typically done according to rank, seniority, family size, and special needs. Additionally, he served on the Embassy Commissary Board, ensuring the embassy's small commissary—about the size of a US 7-Eleven—was effectively managed and appropriately stocked within US government and French regulations.

Perhaps most important of all, Chief Derby advised the defense attaché and attaché team on what was administratively and legally permissible, and more importantly, *not* permissible, in the use of US government vehicles, travel funds, and other US government resources. Since this type of duty was new territory for many military officers (except the Army, which had the armed services' best, and arguably only, bona fide foreign area officer development program), some attachés had become careless or worse, misappropriating government resources—vehicles, time, or people—for their own gain. This was almost always punishable under the Uniform Code of Military Justice (UCMJ) and career-ending or worse.

Under Chief Warrant Officer Derby's tutelage there were four noncommissioned officers: two from the Army and one each from the Air Force and Navy. Much like for commissioned officers, the Army had arguably the best selection and training program for mid-career sergeants who were destined for US embassy duty. The Marines at the embassy, on the other hand, were superbly selected and trained to *secure and defend* US embassies around the world. They typically reported to the embassy's regional security officer, not the defense attaché. The attaché sergeants' training, however, normally involved a combination of language training, as well as classes on the regulations and security requirements that governed attaché support duties.

The final DAO teammate I met on this, my first day at the embassy, was the secretary to the defense attaché, Ms. Rebecca Bouvier. A US citizen, Ms. Bouvier was fluent in French and thoroughly knowledgeable of diplomatic correspondence, office management, and relevant administrative programs and regulations. With the number of absent DAO office team members, it was obvious the DAO had gone to minimum manning levels during this peak French vacation period. This made sense, as there was almost nobody of consequence to do business with over on the French side, and it would remain that way until well into the first week of September.

As we were about to approach the lunch hour, Major Peterson came by my new office and said, "Hey, sir, let me take you around and show you a few more things in the embassy. Then, if you'd like, we can grab lunch in the cafeteria."

"Great," I answered, and we headed out of the office spaces with Eric in the lead.

Working our way down from the third floor, he led me by several key offices, including those of the ambassador, political section (including the political-military, or "pol-mil" officer, whom I would develop a strong professional relationship with), economics section, public affairs, and others. Some, like the consular section and office of defense cooperation, were in a completely different building called the "Talleyrand Building," which was on the other side of the *Hôtel de Crillon* and about 200 meters walking distance from the embassy's main chancery. Given the prominence of this embassy for the US State Department and the United States, a handful of the senior foreign service officers in the embassy held the rank of minister or minister counselor, equivalent to general officer or flag rank for the US Armed Services.

Finally, Major Peterson led me to what I said—only somewhat tongue-in-cheek—I was most interested in seeing: the embassy gym, a modest but effective workout room. Extensive social engagements and the eating and drinking that went with them had been known among attachés to have produced something akin to the college "freshman fifteen," the extra fifteen pounds cafeteria food can add to US university freshmen. But as an Army officer, I had to stay in shape. I would be physically tested bi-annually here, just as I would have been at Fort Sill or Fort Hood or any other Army base: sit-ups, push-ups, and a two-mile run for time. Chief Derby and the two Army sergeants would make darn sure of it, just as they should.

When I was last assigned with troops, as a battalion commander (as well as a brigade and battalion operations officer previous to that), staying in shape was relatively easy. Physical training was scheduled every morning, Monday through Friday, from 0600-0700 hours. As a battalion commander, I would often lead a roughly 500-man battalion on a weekly five- or six-mile run. Now, as an attaché, I would have no required physical training regimen. But I would have frequent contact with people from many nations, including my French counterparts. I settled on an almost daily gym workout during the lunch hour or after-duty hours. The small embassy fitness room, which had been stocked with leftover equipment from US military bases recently shut down in Germany, would be a lifesaver.

After lunch in the embassy cafeteria, Major Peterson and I returned to the DAO spaces. I spent the rest of the afternoon getting "in-processed": establishing email accounts, learning about weekly required meetings, learning how the embassy phones worked, learning local standard operating procedures (SOPs), the best bus lines for me to take home, and obtaining my permanent security badge, among other activities. My sponsor had given me a heads-up on the passport-sized photo needed for the badge, so this was no problem to quickly get squared away.

As I walked out of DAO spaces at about 6:15 p.m., fifteen minutes after the embassy was officially closed, I headed downstairs to the large atrium that preceded the chancery exit. It was at this time that I noticed the two prominent paintings described earlier, of the Marquis de Lafayette and the Comte de Rochambeau. Opposite the paintings, I also spotted a listing, covering the large part of one wall, of all the American ambassadors who had served in Paris over the past 200-plus years. It was a rather select group of just fifty-one names, including US Presidents Thomas Jefferson and James Monroe.

The list also included one name that for probably ninety-nine percent of the diplomats who surveyed the list was a complete unknown: James M. Gavin, who served as Ambassador to France from 1961-1962. To a soldier and student of military history, "Jumpin' Jim" Gavin was a special character. The youngest major general (promoted at age thirty-seven) to command a division in World War II, and the youngest US Army lieutenant general ever, he was also the only US Army general to have made four combat jumps in World War II. The first man to jump into Sicily as a colonel in command of the 505th Parachute Regiment, he also led the 82nd Airborne Division's liberation of the town of *Sainte-Mère-Église*, on D-Day.

Moving on through the main embassy doors, past the still-seated Mr. Franklin and then through Marine Guard Post One and out to the traffic-heavy *Place de la Concorde*, I wondered what it would be like to serve with the current ambassador. Appointed by President Bush as US Ambassador to France, Howard Leach was a very prominent and respected Republican party member from California, as well as a very successful businessman.

Walking on toward the number eighty-four bus stop on the Rue Royale, about a five-minute walk from the embassy and just off the *Place de la Concorde*, I wondered how the next two-plus years under Leach would play out. What would be the major challenges for his ambassadorship to a major US ally? What if President Bush did not get re-elected? I also wondered about the rest of the staff at US Embassy Paris.

New military assignments and missions tend to create new questions, and Paris would prove to be no exception.

CHAPTER 5

FIRST WEEKS

WITH SEPTEMBER HAVING GONE BY in a flash and early October arrived, I was beginning to get well settled in. I had made my first—rather nervous—telephone call over to the French Army staff, hoping the colonel on the other end would understand my school-learned French and that I would understand his native French. Speaking over a telephone, especially in a foreign language, is more difficult than face-to-face, where one can interpret facial expressions, read sincerity, or pick up other nuances. But fortunately, that first, mercifully brief telephone call went well.

I later presented myself to some key French Army staff authorities, particularly Colonel Michel Lanternier, who served as the French Army Chief of Staff's representative to all international military attachés serving in Paris. French Brigadier General Patrice Monpeyssin, who served as the French army staff coordinator for international relations, was also on the list of those contacts I needed to meet early. I would also meet the French Army Chief of Staff General Bernard Thorette a few weeks later.

My first six weeks in Paris had also begun to disprove some US—and perhaps even international—stereotypes of the French people, often perpetrated by made-in-Hollywood movies. Namely, that the French were somewhere between haughty and snobbish, particularly in Paris. This turned out to be pure rubbish. And I'm not describing only the French people of Normandy, where Americans are still revered and welcomed with open arms as if it were the summer of 1944. It was true everywhere my family visited. I silently wished *all* of America could see what I was seeing.

My first strong hint that my Parisian stereotypes might be wrong came during my first days of using the subway, the second busiest in Europe after Moscow's. People were not pushy, and they were cognizant of their—and more importantly, *my*—"personal" spaces. On my first morning exiting the subway platform, a lady just ahead of me went through the creaking metal and glass door before us and did something I totally did not expect: she looked behind her to see if the door needed to be held for the next person. This courteous act would repeat itself hundreds of times during my sojourn in Paris. Other Parisian commuters would instinctively hold the door open for a split-second, without looking back, just in case someone was right behind them.

The same was true of the bus system, where people would give up their seats for the elderly or help a young mother get her stroller onto the bus.

As for those snotty French waiters, I *never* encountered one.

My family was also beginning to settle in. After two weeks in our apartment, in early September, our neighborhood, virtually deserted when we arrived, began to come alive. We soon discovered a tailor shop there, a corner convenience store here, another bakery, and other small businesses we had been unaware of until then. Susan, who had studied French alongside me prior to coming to Paris, and who also spoke excellent Italian and Spanish as well as passable German, was getting to know some of the accompanying spouses and families of the international diplomatic and military community as well. She also began to volunteer her time by running the video room at the American School of Paris in the western Paris suburb of *Garches*, where Erika was now in the fifth grade.

For this first year, we decided to put Maria in a nearby French preschool. It was *very* tough on her, and for about six weeks she did not utter a word of French at home. From our experience, French pre and primary schools were not exactly nurturing places. We heard this later, not only from Americans who had put their children in French schools, but from French parents who had been in the US and now sent their children to local American schools. In every single case, the French children who had attended schools in the US did not want to return to the schools they had previously attended in their native France.

There was, however, a bright side to Maria's school: the *food.* It is no secret that the French take their cuisine seriously, and this starts at a very early age. In preschool, the menus included duck, rabbit, lamb, fish, beef, chicken, and vegetarian options. And this food was not consumed on plastic or with plastic utensils. It was with real silverware on china or faux china. Maria's palate was used to the American delicacies of mac and cheese, chicken wings, French fries, PB&Js, pizza, and pasta, so it was quite the challenge to adapt. Most days, if the menu said she was having duck or fish or lamb, when she asked what she would be having for lunch, we simply said "chicken."

"Chicken? *Again*?" she would ask.

"Yep," we answered.

End of discussion for us, but always the beginning of fine dining for her.

One Saturday in October, Maria finally spoke French. While our family of four was walking along the Seine River, we suddenly heard Maria yell, with a perfect French accent, *"Regard!"* (look!) Thrilled that she had vocalized a word of French, Susan and I did not even look to where she was pointing. We just looked at each other with great relief that Maria had not gone mute from attending a French school. Erika just laughed.

By this point I had also been to several embassy receptions, including my first official reception at the Turkish embassy, which typically kicked off Paris's fall diplomatic reception "season," beginning in early September. When I had visited Paris the previous spring, the outgoing army attaché had advised me to accept all invitations to diplomatic receptions and social events. Colonel Andrew "Andy" Manuele was one service year senior to me. Coincidentally, I had spent two years in the same cadet company as him at West Point.

"Rick, occasionally declining an invitation is not a big deal," Manuele had said. "Sometimes you will have a real scheduling conflict. But having a reputation as someone who habitually does not engage or show up when invited can get you scratched off the list for the rest of your tour, as well as give you—and our DAO team, and even the Army—a bad reputation. And, from a practical perspective, if you ever need something from that embassy or country, you won't exactly be met with open arms."

Colonel Manuele, a bachelor and New Yorker, entertainingly opinionated—but also well-read and informed—had also taught French at West Point. He was highly regarded by the DAO team, the US Embassy leadership, senior French military officers, and French Ministry of Defense officials. His reputation was that of a very effective attaché and US military diplomat. I thought seriously about what he said.

I decided to take the approach he had suggested. If I received a serious invitation—and for me that meant with at least two weeks' notice of an impending event—I would accept it. If it was received with less than a two-week notice, I usually did not take it seriously. This wasn't an ironclad maxim, but I generally assumed, perhaps incorrectly, that it was either someone inviting me because they thought they simply had to, or they had added me at the last moment because their first or second choices had been dropped from the original invitation list. In any case, as most invitations were received four to six, or even eight weeks from an event, I was always suspicious of those that arrived under two weeks from one.

When my tour in Paris—and Army career—would end some

three-plus years after reporting for embassy duty, however, I wondered if I had made the right decision in accepting the vast majority of invitations. The decision to do so was totally mine, but I will not deny that I later harbored some guilt over the nights away from home. Susan often accompanied me, so the girls had a babysitter for two, often three, nights a week. Sometimes I would appear at two or three events in a single evening. Of course, being deployed to a theater of war would have been far tougher on my family.

During the first week of October, I received an invitation that I thought just slightly odd, but I accepted it in any case, because the US defense attaché, Major General Dupré, *wanted* me to accept it. It was a dinner, spouses included, with the French Air Force Chief of Staff, General Richard Wolsztynski, and some select members of his staff.

Why did Dupré encourage me, the Army attaché, to accept a dinner invitation with the senior officer in the French Air Force? It didn't make sense.

CHAPTER 6

FRENCH AIR
FORCE DINNER

AS WE ARRIVED WITH OUR wives at the French Air Force headquarters in the Ballard area of Paris in October 2002, I was still pondering why I, the Army guy, had got the invitation to a high-level dinner with several French Air Force generals, including the five-star (equivalent to four US stars) French Air Force Chief of Staff, General Wolsztysnki.

It certainly made sense for Major General Dupré to be there. He was the relatively new US defense attaché and senior US Air Force officer. It also made sense to invite Colonel Jeffrey Jackson, US air attaché, F-16 Fighting Falcon fighter pilot and Rhodes scholar.

But me? I didn't get it.

I also didn't question Dupré's strong nudge for me to attend, at least not vocally. I never asked him to explain the reason. I would understand it in time, but not for another few weeks.

Meeting the man in charge of the French Air Force, let alone having dinner with him, is no small matter for a military attaché of any country. In 2002 the French Air Force was a formidable—and globally deployed—force. Depending on the factors used for assessment—

quality of pilot training, capabilities of fighter and reconnaissance aircraft, numbers of aircraft, etc.—it was ranked anywhere from sixth to ninth most combat effective in the world at that time. French Mirage fighter aircraft had acquitted themselves well during the 1991 First Gulf War. The previous November, only some nine weeks after 9/11, the French were among the first coalition partners to join the fight against al-Qaeda in Afghanistan, sending ten Mirage fighters to the Hindu Kush.

The recently appointed General Wolsztynski, as I was to discover during the dinner, had attended the US Air Force Academy in Colorado Springs, Colorado. What's more, he attended as the very first French cadet from France's *Ecole de l'air* (Air Force Academy) for one semester as an international exchange cadet. Also present at the dinner was a French lieutenant general (four French, three US stars), Jean-Patrick Gaviard, the J-3 operations officer of the French Joint Staff. A lanky man who stood probably six feet four inches tall, Lieutenant General Gaviard had a boisterous, enthusiastic, and highly engaging demeanor, a good complement to that of his more reserved superior, Wolsztynski. Gaviard, whose height probably stretched the allowable limits for a pilot, had more than 4,000 hours of reconnaissance aircraft flight time, including operational deployments to Africa and Kosovo.

Two brigadier generals and their spouses also sat at our large, round table of fourteen people. Brigadier General Stéphane Abrial had graduated from the French Air Force Academy in 1973, and due to mutual academic credit arrangements at the time, the US Air Force Academy a year later. A fighter pilot, he went on to command the French Air Force's 5th Fighter Squadron in the 1991 Gulf War. Within four years of our dinner he would be promoted three times and become the French Air Force chief of staff. Three years after that he would become the first French officer to serve as commander of NATO Supreme Allied-Command Transformation, replacing a US Marine general named James N. Mattis.

Brigadier General Pascal Vinchon, a fighter pilot who had attended the US Air College, was also there. Brigadier General Vinchon would subsequently serve as the French Defense Attaché to the United States, and later, as a lieutenant general, as the French Military Representative to the NATO Military Committee.

The utility of social events among international allies is occasionally questioned by US lawmakers and perhaps even US citizens, who certainly have every right to ask about the time—either on or off duty—spent this way. However, a couple of congenial, face-to-face hours around a dinner table can enhance military partnerships and networks for years to come. This was a prime example. Over the next ten years, including my time as a Department of Defense civilian, my professional path would cross again and again with all three of the "younger" French generals present on this evening. One significant meeting, which would happen far sooner than I expected, would occur with Lieutenant General Gaviard within a few short weeks.

For the most part, the conversation, mostly in English, was light, especially during the first portion of the meal. The subject of soccer *(football)* was brought up. Somebody lamented France's extremely poor showing in the just-completed summer of 2002 World Cup, held in Japan and South Korea. In 1998, France had won it all, right there in Paris. However, in 2002, the World Champion French National Team, *Les Bleus,* did not even make it out of their first-round bracket.

Not intended as a serious business meeting, the conversation did, however, stray lightly into weightier matters. Someone mentioned the growing civil war in France's former West African colony, the Ivory Coast, where rebels were trying to overthrow President Laurent Gbagbo. Gbagbo had come to power in 2000 after several years of political upheaval in the mid-to-late 1990s, following longtime president Houphouët-Boigny's death in December 1993. Just days prior to our dinner, the conflict had spread and escalated into violent protests in the country's capital, Abidjan. French and international citizens were becoming increasingly at risk in the *Cote d'Ivoire.*

What to do—and what the United States *was doing*—about Iraq and Saddam Hussein was also discussed on the margins. Some two or three weeks prior, President Bush, seeking congressional support for unilateral action against Iraq, had firmly stated to the American people, "The threat from Iraq is unique in the world. It needs the attention of the United States and the world as the greatest Middle East and global threat. The murderous tyrant who has suppressed liberty and freedom in that country for so long must go."

Several Democrats opposed to military action said after the speech that President Bush had not effectively made the case for military action. One of them, questioning the supposed links of al-Qaeda to Iraq, said, "You don't respond to attacks on Pearl Harbor by attacking Peru."

The dinner ended with me still pondering, in the back of my mind, why I was there. It remained a nagging question. *Maybe Major General Dupré is just being inclusive*, I thought. *Or maybe it will all make some sense at some point.*

However, the dinner did drive home a couple of major points with me. The United States, and the US Department of Defense in particular, should never underestimate the impact of our professional military education system, from its military academies, Reserved Officer Training Corps (ROTC), and Officer Candidate School (OCS) commissioning sources through senior service colleges on foreign officers (including noncommissioned officers) and their families. Three of these four senior officers, all except Gaviard, had attended US military schools on some level. Not only did that signal a vote of confidence by the French in the US professional military education system, it also provided the foundation for French and US officers to understand and trust each other more. As Admiral William McRaven, former Commander US Special Operations Command once said, "You can't surge trust."

I believe getting to know someone in a personal and social setting should not be underestimated. I'm not talking about through

Facebook, LinkedIn, or Snapchat. I'm talking about in a face-to-face setting, over a drink, a dinner, or a doughnut.

Diplomacy and communication between nations are very little different from goodwill and understanding between individuals. They are vital in peace and war, no matter the century or decade.

CHAPTER 7

VERDUN

VERDUN, FRANCE, WAS A SCENE of World War I carnage. The sheer numbers boggle the mind: 300,000 French and German dead, and of those, 160,000 unidentified; 30 million artillery shells expended; and 300 days, roughly 10 months, of misery, fear, heroism, and death. Due to the overwhelming magnitude of the casualties and lack of accountability means in that era, the historical numbers vary. Most accounts agree, however, that there were over 360,000 French and almost 340,000 German casualties, dead or wounded, during that third dark year—1916—of the Great War.

On November 11, 2002, I was at Verdun for the US Veterans' Day, and for what many countries in Europe was Armistice Day. US Ambassador to France Howard Leach had asked the DAO where he could visit an "appropriately symbolic place" in France on this day, and Verdun was the recommended place. It would be the first visit to Verdun by a US ambassador to France since World War II. It was practically a foregone conclusion that his defense attaché, Major General Felix Dupré, would accompany him, but not so for me.

When Dupré asked me to join him on this highly symbolic national French holiday marking the end of World War I, I was again a bit surprised. The representational ceremony at Verdun was not such a high-profile public relations mission that it required two senior attachés. But I trusted Dupré completely, so I had no reason to question or deny his invitation.

Born of a US Navy father and French mother, Dupré had lived in France as an adolescent when US military forces were stationed there, until President Charles De Gaulle sent them packing in 1966. So his French accent was superb, and he didn't need a translator for the events at Verdun. He was an optimistic, enthusiastic, and calm leader. I felt comfortable with him in public, or most anywhere for that matter. I decided to make the best of it.

Knowing he and I would serve at least eighteen months more together, I did not want to even mildly screw this up. My baseline public affairs training had taught me, among other things, to always be professional, to talk only about what you *know* (i.e., don't speculate or hypothesize), to always be ready for an off-the-wall question, and, of course, to never compromise your integrity. These baseline approaches and attitudes might not make one the next George C. Marshall or Dwight D. Eisenhower, but they would certainly keep one off the front pages of *LeMonde*, or worse, the *Washington Post*.

My personal international liaison code of conduct, through observation and experience in lower and tactical but similar international assignments with the Germans, Italians, and others, told me to be humble and sincere and to keep a sense of humor. In other words, not to take myself too seriously. Arrogance, or just the perception of it, was detrimental to international liaison duty, especially among soldiers. And I mean the term "soldier" broadly, to include sailors, marines, airmen, and coast guardsmen, including foreign ones. Be perceived as arrogant and you'll be shunned. Be shunned and you're worthless as a US representative, military or otherwise.

The day's weather was emblematic of the wet, mind-numbing, and bone-chilling days from February 21 to December 18, 1916—drizzly, cold, and dreary, with a low cloud cover and light wind. Our day would begin mid-morning at the Douaumont *Ossuary*—roughly translated, "place of bones"—a French name given to the place and structure where the bones of some 130,000 unidentified French and German soldiers are interred.

After Ambassador Leach, Major General Dupré, and I met several local French officials and military officers, we were given a twenty-minute tour of the Ossuary by an Ossuary employee. Our thirtysomething guide's engaging manner was the only refreshing aspect of this very respectfully built yet somber place. It was some 449 feet long, with forty-two alcoves and a 150-foot tower representing an artillery shell in the middle.

There were many engraved dedications on the beige stone walls and ceilings—literally thousands of names of the fallen, paid for by their families. I had been to other battlefields where some semblance of political-military or strategic purpose helped me rationalize the cost in blood and suffering. This was barely so at Verdun. The French and German strategies, if not mantras—to "bleed each other white"—plunged into the most horrific depths of attrition and trench warfare. Ultimately, France, on its own soil and fighting for its national soul, while aided by the British at the Battle of the Somme (in its own right one of the bloodiest battles in history), which relieved pressure on Verdun, held off long enough to recoup previously lost terrain and avoid defeat by the Germans. France, the United States, Great Britain, and their allies would ultimately emerge victorious in the Great War on November 11, 1918.

After the tour, Major General Dupré and I waited for the wreath-laying ceremony to begin outside, where we relished the fresh air, drizzling rain and all. We received word from one of the French officers that one of the official party members for the upcoming wreath ceremony had not yet arrived, apparently due to the bad weather. It turned out to be the regional prefect. Prefects, I later learned, were formidable figures in the French political, judiciary, and law enforcement landscape. Originating from the Napoleonic era, they represent the French central government throughout

France, and possess a wide range of judiciary, law enforcement, and "public order" powers.

The senior *préfets* are assigned by region, each with two to eight *sous-préfets,* depending on the number of departments in the region. They operate under the auspices of the French Ministry of Interior, for which there is no US equivalent. In Europe, Ministries of the Interior are an amalgam of the US Department of Homeland Security, Justice Department, and Federal Bureau of Investigation, a far stretch from the French Ministry of Interior's faux-US friend, the US Department of Interior.

The prefect's arrival at the ceremony would be mildly dramatic, not because of anything he did, but because of the skill of the gendarmes helicopter pilot who brought him to our dreary venue.

"Is that a helicopter I hear, sir?" I somewhat rhetorically asked Dupré as I looked skyward.

"Sure sounds like one," he responded with a look of surprise.

As we looked up toward the low, pea-soup-thick, rain-spitting clouds, now perhaps no more than 200-250 meters above us, we could hear the chopper, but we had no idea where it was. Suddenly, as if lowered by a rappelling rope, the blue-and-white helicopter, with *Gendarmerie* written on the side, descended straight down from the low clouds . . . and landed perfectly on the immaculately tended grass about 100 meters from the Ossuary. General Dupré and I just looked at each other, eyebrows raised, and did not say a word. That was a darned impressive piece of flying.

Ambassador Leach, Major General Dupré, the mayor of the nearby city of Verdun, and several other local French civic leaders and military officers, closed about one-third of the distance to the helicopter and stopped on the edge of the pavement below us. As it audibly decreased its whining engine and rotors, the door popped open, and out stepped a roughly mid-fifties man, representing the French national government. He was wearing a dark blue military uniform with a double-breasted suit jacket and gold buttons on a white shirt with a black four-in-hand knotted tie and gold-trimmed epaulettes. His headgear, which also bore gold embroidery, was of the traditional military "peaked-cap" style. I thought his uniform, if perhaps a bit antiquated, represented authority without being overstated.

The Verdun mayor welcomed the prefect and immediately introduced him to Ambassador Leach and Major General Dupré. He then introduced the prefect to me.

I leaned forward, extended an outreached hand, looked him squarely in the eyes, and said, *"Enchanté, monsieur le préfet."*

He responded with a simple *"Bonjour, mon colonel"* and met the rest of our party.

For a moment or two thereafter, I wondered if *"Enchanté"* (directly translated, "enchanted" or "enamored" but also meaning "delighted" or "happy") was the best response. Saying "enchanted"— or what sounded like it to me—to a senior public official did not feel right. *Perhaps in my earlier days, had I ever met a young French girl, sure,* Enchanté *would have been appropriate,* I thought.

After a few months in France, depending on the person, I changed my greeting to something acceptable for the occasion but which I could feel more comfortable with, such as *"Je suis très heureux de faire votre connaissance"* (I am very pleased to make your acquaintance) or the abbreviated *"très heureux"* or *"c'est un plaisir"* (It's a pleasure).

From our meeting place our group was led by a gentleman who turned out to be the museum's curator to a spot about fifty meters from Ossuary's main entrance and down some steps to a paved platform. Standing on that platform, with the Ossuary to our backs, we could look out and see thousands of simple, white crosses. On the platform were perhaps fifty folding chairs, most already filled with people.

After a very brief introduction by a French gendarmes lieutenant colonel, the prefect gave a mercifully short speech, about fifteen minutes, without a single note. Upon its conclusion, the curator then motioned for others, who had already been pre-briefed during their walk from the helicopter to the venue, to line up. As they did, other senior officials, including Dupré in the front and me slightly behind him, did so as well.

At the appointed signal, the entire group walked up to a designated spot near the edge of the platform, where we were guided by a French Army sergeant, and jointly placed several wreaths outside of the Ossuary. Upon the completion of placing the wreaths, the Marseillaise was played. All saluting eyes faced the large French flag flying atop a long, white, and dominating pole set in the middle of the cemetery. A massive bell in the Ossuary's tower then tolled its solemn, deep peals over the thousands of crosses in the cemetery behind us.

CHAPTER 8

NEXT MISSION

AS THE OSSUARY *DOUAUMONT* MEMORIAL event concluded, I caught myself again wondering why I was there for what was essentially a window-dressing appearance. I rationalized that our dual appearance conveyed that the United States, a major French ally, took this day and our French allies seriously. We did, after all, send over two million American doughboys to serve in Europe during the Great War, with over one million fighting side by side with the French, Belgian, British, and other forces. Of those, 116,708 Americans would make the ultimate sacrifice. Consequently, over 33,000 were interred on French or British soil, as requested by their immediate family members or next of kin.

Departing the Ossuary *Douaumont*, we made the roughly forty-five-minute drive over to the US Meuse-Argonne cemetery, located northwest of Verdun and just east of the village of *Romagne-sous-Montfaucon*. The largest US cemetery in Europe and North Africa, and one of ten in Europe from World War I, most of the 14,246 who are buried there fought in the great Meuse-Argonne Offensive.

Meticulously maintained by the American Battle Monuments Commission (ABMC), upon driving through the cemetery's large white marble gates, Dupré and I were soon struck by the perfectly aligned and pristine white marble crosses, set on perfectly manicured grounds. *This solemn yet magnificent blending of marble and greenery would make even the groundskeepers of Arlington Cemetery tip their hats,* I thought.

The overwhelming feeling was one of sanctity and respect. Then both Dupré and I realized, nearly simultaneously, we had been "here" before.

"I remember visiting one of these cemeteries as a kid," he remarked.

"So do I, sir," I replied, surprising myself with the just-emerged memory in my mind's eye. "My dad was a sergeant in the Army, just across the French-German border in Kaiserslautern," I said. "As I recall, he took my mother, little brother, and me to the US cemetery nearest to Metz, France."

For some reason the name of "Metz" was stuck in my head. Being nine years old at the time, however, I could not recall the name of the American cemetery nearest that frontier World War I French town. I could only visualize the many white crosses, dimmed by the mental haze of about thirty-seven years' passing. *This is a vision which not even 100 years of living will snuff out,* I thought.

"How about you, sir? Which cemetery did you visit?" I asked.

"The one I most remember is Suresnes, the one in Paris," said General Dupré. "The thing that stands out about that cemetery is that so many died from that terrible Spanish influenza. What a hell of a thing, to live through the death and destruction of 'the war to end all wars,' only to be felled on foreign soil by one of the worst flu epidemics known to man."

As we pulled up to the visitor's center at the Meuse-Argonne Cemetery, we were met by a man I thought in his mid-fifties. He wore the uniform common to all of the ABMC cemetery superintendents across Europe. Minus all the gold trim, it looked rather similar to that of a French prefect.

We soon learned that, like other superintendents throughout the ABMC-Europe cemeteries, Joseph Phillip "Phil" Rivers spoke the local language fluently. Also like several other ABMC superintendents, he had served in the US armed forces first. Our Air Force had sent him to Germany in the late 1960s for what was supposed to be a four-year tour. While stationed there he met his French wife, and, as it often does, love motivated him to improve his French. In January 1976, he began working for ABMC and subsequently became the Superintendent of the Brittany, Oise-Aisne, Normandy, and Meuse-Argonne cemeteries.

After brief self-introductions, Rivers said, "Follow me, gentlemen," and led us to a magnificent Romanesque stone edifice on the high ground overlooking a sea of white crosses. As we approached the entrance, below us we could see clusters of people beginning to gather, perhaps sixty or seventy in all, with mostly French flags and one distinct American flag in our sights. Entering through what must have been a twenty-foot-high massive door, inside we beheld a sparkling marble-inlaid chapel, perhaps large enough for a service of forty or so people. Behind the modest altar were the national flags of the World War I victors.

"The stained-glass windows reflect the unit insignias of the units who fought here," Rivers noted, "and the ground we are standing on was captured by the US 32nd Infantry Division. Those doughboys were mostly from Michigan and Wisconsin. The French named them *Les Terribles*, and they were also known as the Red Arrow Division," he concluded.

As Dupré and I left the chapel, I suspected we were both asking our military consciences the same question: how tough it must have been for these mostly very young men to have voyaged for weeks by train and ship and train again, and finally by foot, to find themselves on these hellish French battlefields. Once here, if they were lucky, they might get a letter or two from home before meeting their Maker. By some miracle, they might even survive the inferno that was the Great War.

As we headed down a wide set of stone stairs to the designated ceremonial stone tile platform below, Superintendent Rivers provided more details on the hallowed ground we were on. "This cemetery also includes naval rail-gunners and members of the lesser known American expedition to Russia," he said. "Also buried here are African-American soldiers of the 92nd and 93rd Divisions, as well as women, civilians, and even children. Nine Medal of Honor recipients are interred here, too, the most of any cemetery in Europe. One of them, Freddie Stowers, is the only African-American to receive the Medal of Honor in World War I."

Reaching the bottom of the steps, Rivers led us through the milling crowd to the front of the venue, where we met several local officials, including mayors of nearby towns, a fire chief, a gendarmes lieutenant colonel, a French Army colonel, and the head of a local French veterans group. On the edge of the stone platform where we were standing, I noticed a US color guard representing the Army, Marines, Navy, and Air Force. There were also three French flag bearers, two from local fire departments and another from a local French veterans' organization.

After the French and US national anthems, and a brief welcome by a civilian representative of the ABMC headquarters in Paris, a few speeches were given. Then, at Rivers' signal, eight officials, including Leach and Dupré, laid their hand-carried wreaths on small stands at the edge of the platform. The wreaths were more like large bouquets of flowers. As we stepped back from them, a bugler, standing on the side of the hill by the chapel, played taps. Then Dupré and I proceeded to shake the hands of every flag bearer and French veteran who had participated in the ceremony.

After saying farewell to Rivers, we walked up to our car and drove off the 130-acre sacred grounds, headed for the village of Verdun. We had another ceremony to participate in. It would be roughly similar to the previous two, with one exception: it would involve about a 350-yard walk, with Leach, the mayor, the prefect, Dupré, and me leading our group of about a dozen, followed by several flag bearers, from near the *Port Chausee* and an iconic Verdun fortress (from which the

US Army Corps of Engineers insignia is said to be designed) to the *Monument de la Victoire*—the Victory Memorial.

To my surprise the march was lined with several hundred onlookers, many of whom were at the Victory Memorial end. About two-thirds of the way along, I heard, "Hey, Rick!" Looking over my shoulder, I saw Colonel Paul Reynolds, a West Point classmate and Army surgeon serving in Germany. I had not seen Paul in the twenty-four years since our commissioning as second lieutenants.

Finally getting to our place of lodging early that evening, near the center of Verdun and not far from the Meuse River and Verdun's cathedral, we met our family members. It was rare that we would bring family along on official events such as this. However, since November 11, 2002 fell on a Monday, it allowed for easy travel to Verdun on Saturday and an opportunity to visit this historical town before the official events on Monday.

That evening, as part of our dinner, we celebrated Maria's fifth birthday. She had been born in a German hospital in Aschaffenburg when I was a field artillery battalion commander at nearby Babenhausen. About six weeks before her birth, the German doctor who would deliver her had projected she would be born on November 11. I told him no way was that going to happen.

"Why do you say that?" he asked, with an excellent American accent.

"Two reasons: you doctors almost always get this day wrong [Erika's projected birthdate was off by about ten days], *and* it would be too cool if she was born on November 11. That is the American Veteran's Day. What a wonderful gift she would be for this veteran to celebrate on that day and every Veteran's Day."

November 11, of course, the day the World War I armistice was signed, signified something totally different to this late middle-aged German man. He forced a wry smile nonetheless, without further response.

Susan and I had to get the kids back to Paris for school early the next morning, so we decided to call it an early evening. Dupré then asked me to accompany him up the steps to his hotel room, one floor higher than mine. As we got to the top of the steps leading to his floor, I could see the pensive look in his eyes, as if there was something he had been meaning to get off his chest.

"Rick," he said with some hesitation, "I am not long for Paris."

I paused for a moment to process what he had just said, but my response was still perplexed. "What? What do you mean, sir? You practically just got here." I was anticipating bad news, perhaps an illness in the family or something else unfortunate.

"Well," he continued, "the secretary of defense no longer wants a general officer in Paris. And when I leave, I want you to replace me."

CHAPTER 9

INSIDE BASEBALL

AS SUSAN AND I DROVE back to Paris with the girls early on Tuesday morning, the 12th of November, it was beginning to make sense why Dupré had asked me to accompany him on the two events. He was setting me up to replace him. He must have known a change in the DAO leadership was in the works. I did not yet know when that might occur, but I now knew it was clearly a possibility. When I thought the time was right, I would ask him about it. Would it be weeks, or months? *I'll know soon enough,* I thought.

Admittedly, while I believed Dupré was a great leader and ideally suited for the defense attaché post in Paris, I was intrigued and energized at the prospect of being the defense attaché. Paris had one of only three US embassies, in 2002, where a general or flag officer served as defense attaché. The others were in Beijing and Moscow. As far as US Army foreign area officer service went, one of these three posts was the pinnacle of service to the nation.

Meanwhile, as the weeks went by, the US military buildup was increasing in the Middle East. Saddam Hussein had essentially been boxed in by a constant and costly US military air presence in the region since the 1991 Gulf War. Media reports had conveyed he had or was developing weapons of mass destruction. Just three days prior to our Verdun event, the UN Security Council adopted Resolution 1441, stating Iraq had remained "in material breach" of past resolutions and giving it a "final opportunity to comply with its disarmament obligations" set out by the council's own resolutions stretching back to the end of the 1991 Persian Gulf War.

The UN and International Atomic Energy Agency's powers to conduct inspections throughout Iraq were increased, and Iraq was notified it must allow "immediate, unimpeded, unconditional, and unrestricted access" to "facilities, buildings, equipment, records, and means of transport which they wish to inspect." Weapons inspections began anew on November 27, 2002.

Resolution 1441 also warned that Iraq would face "serious consequences" if it failed to comply with its disarmament obligations. On December 7, 2002, Iraq submitted its declaration "of all aspects of its [weapons of mass destruction] programs" that Resolution 1441 required. The declaration was supposed to have provided information on any prohibited weapons activity since UN inspectors left the country in 1998. The resolution required the declaration to be "currently accurate, full, and complete," but UN and IAEA inspectors informed the UN Security Council on December 19 that the declaration had contained "little new information."

That same day, US Secretary of State Colin Powell stated that the Iraqi declaration contained a "pattern of systematic gaps" that demonstrated evidence of "another material breach" of Iraq's disarmament requirements. From where I sat, it looked like the US was methodically building a case for another war, one that would ostensibly resolve the Iraq—and Saddam Hussein—problem once and for all.

In mid-January 2003, we received a late notice US Embassy Paris visit from a senior US Air Force general in the European theater. His military aide had scheduled an office call for him with Dupré, who knew him well, and me, before he flew on to Africa. It was the first instance in my military service that I had heard a very senior officer speak so frankly, openly questioning US policy in the Middle East, particularly with respect to the ongoing buildup around Iraq. He confided in both Dupré and me.

"Gentlemen, I hate to say this," he said, "but it seems this administration is just spoiling for a fight, just looking for ways to start another war with Iraq—or finish what was not accomplished in 1991. And I'm not at all sure we need to, or should, go there. While we might find WMDs tomorrow, and they might have been there at one time, we have yet to locate any." He paused. "I'm sure as heck no politician, but I don't think we have the slightest clue of what is going to come after Saddam Hussein, if we do in fact end up toppling that SOB."

This was the first "inside baseball" commentary about what was brewing in Washington D.C. and on the borders of Iraq that I had heard, and I presumed Dupré had heard as well, over the previous few months. It was also slightly unsettling (but much appreciated by me), even if said confidentially, from a seasoned, combat-experienced, and highly respected US Air Force fighter pilot and general. This was one of the first signs for me that the upcoming war was not going to be the same as the 1991 Gulf War, when American military forces, joined by a far-ranging and robust international coalition, crushed Iraqi military forces in just over four days.

And the general's insights gave me pause as I suddenly realized the scope of what could be my next duty position.

CHAPTER 10

SECRETARY POWELL AT THE UN

ON THE MORNING OF FEBRUARY 6, 2003, I was at the French *École de Guerre* (School of Warfare), inside the grand French *École Militaire* complex facing the Eiffel Tower from the southeast end of the Champ de Mars, the spacious grassy area at the base of the Tower. The *École Militaire* had been established in 1750 and had had a young and brilliant cadet named Napoleon Bonaparte as a student. It now contained several offices, classrooms, and even a large outdoor horse stable and riding area.

When the Paris International Military Attaché Association, including over 170 international attachés assigned to Paris, would meet as a group to hear from senior French government officials, it was at the *École Militaire* where we would officially meet. It was also home to General Henri Bentégeat, who, like General Thorette, was a *troupe de marine* (French US marine equivalent) and Chief of Defense, the highest-ranking uniformed officer in the French Armed Forces. In the United States Armed Forces, he would be called the chairman of the Joint Chiefs of Staff.

I had just left the office of US Colonel Hank Allen, the liaison officer from the US Army's Training and Doctrine Command to its sister French organization. I noticed several French majors, perhaps twenty feet away from me, attending classes at the *Ecole Militaire*. Just before I entered a classroom, one of them must have recognized I was a US military attaché by my US Army service green uniform and the gold aiguillettes (braided cords) draping down from my left shoulder.

Stopping about thirty feet down the hallway, and in a voice loud enough for his five or six nearby peers to hear, the French officer asked me rather sardonically, "*So*, do you *really* believe all of that *stuff* that your secretary of state said at the United Nations yesterday?"

I quickly responded, loud enough for the French officer, his group, and anybody behind them to hear: "Of course I do! That was *General Colin Powell* speaking! Why would I doubt *him*? Why would *anyone* doubt him? Didn't you see the evidence that he presented?"

The major just shook his head and entered the classroom, followed by the other students.

What a smart-ass, I thought. *Who is he to question Colin Powell? Surely, General Colin Powell would never compromise his integrity. The evidence that he portrayed to the United Nations and the world looked pretty convincing to me.*

When he had been in the Army, Colin Powell had been widely respected as a competent, effective, and fair leader. I distinctly remember him speaking to my Command and General Staff College course, taking off his Army "Class A" green coat, draping it over the podium, and immediately connecting with my classmates and me. Of course, during Operations Desert Shield and Desert Storm, he had his differences with General "Stormin'" Norman Schwarzkopf, the Commander of US and allied troops in the theater. And yet, both men worked well together.

Some thought Powell to have become more of a "political" general (which is somewhat redundant for generals of four-star rank), but the respect for him remained. Heck, in the late 1990s he was considered one of the most—if not *the* most—respected people in America. Many Americans thought he could have been elected president then. *There's no way in hell Colin Powell would sell out,* I thought.

That night, after reading articles from the *Washington Post* and the *New York Times*, I had seen my sentiments corroborated, or so I thought. Both publications ran articles agreeing that Powell had presented a pretty darn good—if not irrefutable—case at the UN. Some of the French and international news outlets, however, were not convinced.

"Ah, they're just being their typically independent, occasionally out-of-touch French selves," I concluded.

Or were they?

CHAPTER 11

IN CHARGE

DEPARTING MY *RUE DE PRONY* apartment early on Monday, February 25, 2003, I decided to take the subway. To enhance personal security, I was trying to remain unpredictable, so today I would leave the apartment a bit earlier and take the metro, instead of one of the two or three bus lines that I could also take in the area. It was chilly, even for Paris in late February. That would only last, however, until I got to the warmer subway, which today would take me right to the Place de la Concord. From there, it was a short walk to the embassy from the metro's exit near the Hotel *Crillon*.

Just days prior, here at the *Place de la Concorde*, there had been somewhere between 100,000 and 200,000 protesters gathered against a possible war with Iraq. That was small peanuts compared to Rome, which had over three million people in what the 2004 *Guinness Book of World Records* would later call the largest protest event in human history. Globally, fifteen million people were said to have protested the looming war in the Middle East.

Things were also heating up on the increasingly divided international political front. The United States, United Kingdom, and Spain had co-sponsored a Security Council resolution, stating "Iraq has failed to take the final opportunity afforded to it by Resolution 1441."

For their part, Russia and France submitted a memorandum that military force should be a "last resort," and that force should not yet be used because there was "no evidence" that Iraq possessed weapons of mass destruction. It also stated, however, that "inspections . . . cannot continue indefinitely. Iraq must disarm." It further added that Baghdad's cooperation, although improving, was not "yet fully satisfactory." The French-Russian memorandum also proposed a new timeline requiring regular reporting to the Security Council about inspectors' progress, as well as a progress report to be submitted 120 days after the program of work was adopted. The UN did not adopt either measure. It was becoming increasingly clear that the United States and France were not on the same page when it came to Iraq.

On February 14, the chief UN weapons inspector, Hans Blix, had reported that no WMDs had been found in Iraq. Yes, there had been traces of chemical weapons, like mustard gas, most likely from Saddam Hussein's gassing of the Kurds in 1988. However, the United States and the UN were not at all surprised by those. Other than a few empty artillery shells, there was no evidence of actual WMDs or of a systemic program for producing them.

On the same day that Blix spoke at the UN, so did France's Foreign Minister, Mr. Dominique Villepin. He noted the inspections were achieving results, and he appealed for more time for the UN and IAEA inspectors. Villepin also declared that war should be an absolute last resort, and that the international community was not convinced armed conflict was the next step.

Villepin stated, "War might seem to produce the swiftest results, but let us not forget that having won the war, peace will have to be built. Let us not be deluded by this. It will be an extremely difficult process to preserve Iraq's unity, and to restore stability in an enduring way, given a country harshly damaged by the use of military force."

After I walked into Dupré's office for his weekly Monday 9:00 a.m. meeting with the principal attachés, the focus was on the previous week's events and potential French military preparations for joining the forming coalition in Iraq. At this stage, the term "coalition of the willing" had not fully come into vogue, but the developing coalition in Iraq was being discussed that way. It was clear that no matter what was to occur in the weeks ahead, the US buildup in Iraq was falling far short of that which was achieved in 1991 for Desert Storm.

As for the French Armed Forces, we had gotten word in January from our contact at the French Joint Staff that the French were serious about building a strong military contingent for potential actions in Iraq. Central to it would be the French 7th Armored Brigade, including over 120 Leclerc main battle tanks and associated infantry and field artillery. In all, this task force would have provided over 7,000 troops. French options also being developed included roughly 9,000 troops, as well as a massive deployment approaching 15,000 troops.

As our meeting concluded, Dupré asked me to stay behind.

"Rick," he began, "this Thursday will be my last day as the DATT. I'll be around in the city next week, shipping my household effects and car, so if you need anything, I'll still be within arm's reach. However, as of this Friday, you are in charge. SECDEF personally approved your selection to be the defense attaché. The ambassador and deputy chief of mission know and approve. I will call everyone together in the DAO this afternoon to let them know, and the ambassador will announce it at Wednesday's country team meeting. Congratulations."

General Dupré extended his hand to me, and we shook.

"Thanks for your trust in me, sir," I said. "It has been an honor serving with you."

Although I was certainly going to miss Felix and Lin Dupré, who had done a terrific job leading our attaché team as a couple, I felt honored to have been selected, and I relished the leadership challenge. However, given the political-military turbulence swirling around France, Europe, and the United States concerning Iraq, I was a bit pensive as to how this might develop.

Before leaving his office, Dupré informed me he had already set up a series of meetings and introductions, including with the

French chief of defense and senior MOD officials, just one level below the minister of defense, Madame Michèle Alliot-Marie. I would meet her later. The next day, he informed me, we would begin the introductions, already scheduled with the French Navy chief of staff (US chief of naval operations equivalent), whose office was the closest to the embassy.

At that first meeting, as with every other meeting with a French military service chief, Dupré tried to put a positive spin on his departure, focusing more on his being *called* to a new assignment rather than the US downgrading the defense attaché position, and by extension the US-France military relationship writ large. All of the French service chiefs, including the chief of defense, General Bentégeat, were quite gracious in their responses. Only one, however, belied that grace with a look somewhere between annoyed and doubtful: Admiral Jean-Louis Battet, the chief of staff of the Navy. Try as he might to nod understandingly, I perceived Admiral Battet expected there was more to the story than just Dupré being reassigned.

I decided to schedule meetings with the ambassador, deputy chief of mission, and political counselor (considered a diplomatic two-star general equivalent at US Embassy Paris), to get their guidance and thoughts on how we could best serve together. Fortunately, I had already begun to work closely with one of the political officers, Jeremy Brenner. Jeremy had to frequently write reports—"cables"—back to the State Department to keep top officials informed of the political-military front in France, and I was more than happy to help him, no matter who got the credit. I would end up in a very similar relationship with his successor, Susan Bremner.

CHAPTER 12

CHARM SCHOOL VISITS PARIS

ON THE FOLLOWING MONDAY IN early March, 2003, at 0900, I led our Defense Attaché Office leadership team meeting, as usual. But I asked everyone—attaché assistants, operations sergeants, secretaries, and drivers—to be present. I began by acknowledging what a tremendous job Major General Dupré had done in leading our team during the previous six-plus months. We had been most fortunate to have had him lead us for the time he did. He clearly had begun to close some rifts between the DAO and other offices in the embassy, including the ambassador's.

I let the team know, however, the DAO's relationship with other embassy offices was an area in which we still had work to do. My leadership motto had long been "One Team, One Fight," but now I would intend for it to include *everyone* in the embassy. In the end, if we made the ambassador, DCM and other embassy colleagues successful, then we'd all be successful.

I also let everyone know how honored I was to lead and work with them, and that the US naval attaché, Captain Deak Childress, or the air attaché, Colonel Jeffrey Jackson, both highly experienced and respected professionals, could just as well have been picked for this job.

"I honestly have no clue why I got the nod, except for the fact that the next flag officer after Major General Dupré to have taken the job should have been an Army general," I informed them. "I guess it was just the Army's turn."

I also emphasized I was not big on meetings. We would have two per week. The first, at 9:00 a.m. on Mondays, would never go beyond an hour and would include the principal attachés and the chief of the office of defense cooperation, Colonel Dorothea Cypher-Erickson. The second, on Thursday morning, would be a stand-up meeting not to exceed ten minutes.

"Give me your top two priorities or issues for that meeting," I informed them, "and nothing more."

After bringing up a few more priority items, I adjourned the meeting after twenty minutes. With people walking out of my office, my assistant Army attaché walked up to me. Lieutenant Colonel William "Bill" Cosby had served as a field artillery officer with the US Berlin Brigade, 1st Infantry Division and 101st Airborne Division,.

"Sir, I just wanted to remind you that I'll be out this afternoon assisting the generals and admirals who will be here as part of charm school," Cosby said.

Charm school was the colloquial moniker in place of the more formal *capstone general and flag officer course.*

This course, a sort of professional finishing school for newly promoted generals and admirals or soon-to-be promoted colonels and Navy captains, supported all military services. It was managed by the National Defense University at historic Fort Lesley J. McNair, located on the Potomac River in Washington, D.C. With a focus on ethics and senior leadership, it was a five-week course, which typically included at least one week overseas. The newly promoted general officers and admirals could pick the locations to where they wanted to travel. Often, to broaden their situational awareness, they chose places they knew little about, or theaters of operation they might soon be assigned to.

"Bill, how many officers will be here tomorrow?" I asked.

"There are about a dozen, sir, from four services—Army, Navy, Air Force, and Marines—as well as one civilian senior executive. They'll be accompanied by a retired Air Force four-star."

As I nodded affirmatively, Cosby continued, "And oh, by the way, I'd appreciate it if you could open our session with them."

I normally preferred more than a few hours' notice before speaking to generals and admirals, especially having just assumed a new responsibility. I nonetheless confirmed I would be there.

"Sure, Bill, no problem. It'll be my pleasure. Who else is expected to address them?" I asked.

"Well, they will likely hear from either the ambassador or deputy chief of mission or their representative; the chief, office of defense cooperation, or her representative; and representatives from the political and economics offices."

"Okay, I'll be there."

We had been pretty busy the previous week, focusing on the transition between Dupré and me, and I didn't recall the capstone Course visit ever coming up. *I'll be ready, nonetheless,* I thought.

The next morning, with a few minutes to go before the start of the meeting, I stood outside of an embassy briefing room as the capstone entourage arrived. Leading them was Cosby, who was normally unflappable but now looked a bit anxious, along with their senior mentor, a retired US Air Force four-star general, who I estimated to be in his late sixties or so.

"Sir," Cosby said, nodding to the general, "this is Colonel Rick Steinke, the Defense Attaché."

"Pleased to meet you, Colonel," said the general.

"My pleasure to meet you, sir. We look forward to a good discussion with this exceptional group," I said.

As the general turned to enter the briefing room, Cosby leaned in and said in as low a voice as he could, "Sir, heads-up. We have an Army brigadier general who has been a real pain. He is not happy."

Within seconds of this warning, a brigadier general, whom we'll call Adams spoke up. "Hey, Colonel, do you think you could have done better with our accommodations?"

With *our accommodations*? What was he talking about?

"Seems I'm livin' in a *construction zone*," continued Adams.

After glaring at me and then Cosby for a second or two, he walked into the briefing room. *What was* that *about?* I asked myself.

As I turned to look at Cosby, he quickly shot back, "Sir, they are staying in the four-star hotel we normally book for our VIPs, the one about four to five blocks from here and that gives the US government temporary duty lodging rate. However, they did some work there over the past couple of days, and there is some noise along with a bit of occasional dust."

"Well, did any of that dust get into his room?"

"Not that I am aware of."

"And what time did the workers stop yesterday?"

"When I got everybody to their rooms in the late afternoon, a small crew was just finishing up. Unless Adams laid right down to take a nap, he couldn't have lost more than a few minutes of sleep due to any noise, because the workers were gone not long thereafter."

"Did anybody else complain about the hotel?"

"*Nobody* did."

"Okay. No sweat."

I was familiar with the boutique hotel where the generals and admirals were staying. As Cosby stated, it had a four-star rating. It was frequently used by international businessmen, as well as the embassy protocol office for lodging VIPs or other embassy visitors. Furthermore, due to a deal negotiated by the embassy, the hotel gave a great rate to US government travelers on official business, ensuring that it did not exceed the maximum allowable lodging reimbursement for Paris. That was almost unheard of for hotels of this class in Paris, especially in the eighth *Arrondisement*, just off the *Place Madeleine* and not far from the *Place de la Concorde*. Most travelers would pay more than 300 dollars per night for this hotel, but because the embassy was a consistent customer, it got a reduction in rates of about thirty to thirty-five percent.

As I moved into the briefing room to take a spot at the large, rectangular oak table, I could see Adams carrying on with another Army brigadier general. We'll call him Costello. Both were in animated conversation, while everyone else, including the retired four-star general, were facing my way and ready to get the presentations started.

To get the two kibitzing generals to quiet down, I raised my voice slightly and said, "Gentlemen, if we could start now, I will provide an initial scene-setter discussing the overall status and key aspects of the French Armed Forces, and then I'll turn it over to my partner and representative from the Office of Defense Cooperation, who will talk about the security cooperation and foreign military sales cases we have with our French counterparts."

For the next fifteen minutes or so, I provided the officers as concise yet comprehensive an overview of the French Armed Forces that I could, to include force numbers in the major military services, budget expenditures, new armament systems developments, where the French forces were deployed globally (e.g., Afghanistan, South America, and in relatively significant numbers, Africa, and elsewhere), and where US military forces had ongoing operations with them, such as Afghanistan and Djibouti.

I highlighted that the USS *Cole* had been attacked some two years prior, in October 2000, off the coast of Yemen, in Aden harbor. The attack had killed seventeen American sailors and injured thirty-nine. The *Cole*'s captain later declared that if it wasn't for the French military hospital in Djibouti and the French's positive and prompt response, at least two more would have lost their lives.

I would later give similar briefings to visits by class groups of roughly a dozen students from the senior service colleges (e.g.,

Army War College, National War College), composed of officers in the ranks of lieutenant colonel and colonel (and their Navy, Coast Guard, and civilian equivalents), as well as congressional delegations (CODELs) visiting the embassy. All but one that would follow went extremely well—and that one involved a Texas congressman asking some very presumptuous and loaded questions. This, my first, was not as pleasant as the rest.

As I spoke, I could see all others actively listening, but the two brigadier generals were somewhere between annoyed and bored. After informing the group that we would take questions at the end, I turned it over to an Air Force lieutenant colonel, speaking on behalf of the Embassy's Office of Defense Cooperation.

He began talking about a US foreign military sales case with the French involving binoculars, to which Costello gruffly interrupted, "So, what you're saying is we have a deal with the French over some *binoculars*. Seriously? Wow!" he exclaimed with dripping sarcasm. "Now *that* is really *serious* international defense cooperation!"

Attempting to normalize the conversation, an Air Force general quickly followed Costello's comment in a very measured and reasonable tone. "Well, I know we are also looking at deals with the French concerning aerial refueling platforms and additional airlift capability."

"That is correct," responded the Air Force lieutenant colonel, outlining those and a couple of other security programs our Office of Defense Cooperation was working on with the French.

As the briefing concluded, other generals and admirals presented reasonable and thoughtful questions. As for the two brigadier generals—from *my* service, for Pete's sake—I did not quite know what to think. I believed the Army usually did an excellent job selecting its general officers. I fervently believed what US Army Lieutenant General (Ret.) Terry Scott once told me at Harvard University: the US Army is a meritocracy. No matter your background, you have to earn every promotion.

I wondered, however, if these two new generals had consumed the anti-French Kool-Aid beginning to be served back home, particularly since the recent French foreign minister speech at the UN. Were they reading, sycophant-like, the tea leaves of the rumored disdain of the French by Secretary Rumsfeld? As the morning session ended, all I could think was, *If it's charm school, it's sure as heck not working for these two officers.* Rank itself engenders respect in a meritocracy, yet it doesn't mean that all who hold high rank merit that respect.

Several months later, Brigadier General Costello would be specifically brought to my attention by the French Joint Staff through our liaison officer, Major Kulmayer. Seems Costello was undermining French leadership of ongoing coalition operations in the Balkans. When I found out about this, through official but subdued channels, I was incredulous. But what could I do? I took action in the best way I knew how: by sending a message to him through our US liaison officer to the French Joint Staff, informing him of French frustrations and recommending he stop his behavior—if the reports were indeed true—before it garnered unwanted and very high-level American attention. That seemed to work, as I never again heard anything about him from the French.

CHAPTER 13

DEFENSE ATTACHÉ: WEEK ONE

AS MY FIRST FULL WEEK as defense attaché concluded, except for the dustup with the two brigadier generals of the capstone course, I was thinking that it had been a pretty good one. Chaired by Ambassador Leach, I had attended my first "country team" meeting. The meeting was moderated by Deputy Chief of Mission Alex Wolfe, and it included over twenty representatives of the US Foreign Service and various US government agencies and departments working in US Embassy Paris. The meeting also included the senior foreign service officers representing the political, economics, consular (passports, visas), management, protocol, and public diplomacy sections, and others, as well as those outside of the State Department, including the Federal Bureau of Investigation, Secret Service, Internal Revenue Service, Federal Aviation Administration, Transportation Security Administration, and American Battle Monuments Commission.

As I was getting ready to head out of the office on Friday afternoon, thankful that weekends were generally off limits for diplomatic engagements and looking forward to a quiet weekend with Susan,

Erika, and Maria, the air attaché, Colonel Jeff Jackson, popped his head through my office door.

"Rick," he began, "I got a fax earlier this afternoon from Headquarters, US Air Forces in Europe. I followed that up with a phone call to make sure I understood everything correctly." US Air Forces in Europe, USAFE for short, had headquarters at Ramstein, Germany.

"Okay, and . . . ?" I responded.

"USAFE, I suspect with the urging of US Transportation Command, needs you to request, negotiate, or whatever it takes to get the French to lower the notification time it takes for US military aircraft to enter the French national airspace. The Air Force leadership is asking that you get the current warning time requirement to be lowered from twenty-four hours down to six hours. This issue mainly involves US military aircraft traversing French air space from US air and naval bases in Europe to the Middle East . . . and back," said Colonel Jackson.

It was obvious from official reports—and certainly the news— that the steam toward military action against Iraq was increasing. US forces had gone through a significant regional buildup, which now included the British, Spanish, Polish, and other coalition partners . . . but not the French nor the Germans. Now, it seemed, we needed to be able to step it up in terms of either US transport, reconnaissance, or combat aircraft bound for the Iraqi theater from Europe.

"Jeff, do you have any idea where I ought to make that request? Do we go to the French Air Force? The Ministry of Defense? Or perhaps the French equivalent of our Federal Aviation Administration?" I had to admit that I was clueless. "And when does USAFE need an answer by?"

"They want an answer no later than close of business next Thursday," Jackson responded.

I, of course, knew that answer would come only as quickly as I would be able to present it and, moreover, as quickly as the French government wanted to give it. Given the US-France political tension after the French foreign minister's speech at the UN, the French might even choose to slow-roll me, not answering for days or weeks.

"Okay, if you wouldn't mind, I need you to do some homework before you leave tonight," I said. "Use the best contacts you know to find out who on the French side this request needs to be submitted to. In any case, I'm sure it will end up in the prime minister's office, and most likely reach the president, as well."

"Roger that, Rick. If I get a solid answer tonight, I'll call you at home, or I'll let you know first thing Monday morning," Jackson concluded.

I waited for the answer. It came soon enough.

CHAPTER 14

THE
NEGOTIATION

AS I ENTERED THE DAO and headed to my office on Monday morning, Jackson was there waiting for me. After some pleasant conversation about the weekend, we got down to business. "The person you have to see to get the French to reduce their notification times for entering their air space," he said, "is Lieutenant General Jean-Patrick Gaviard."

"What a minute. I presume you *do* mean the General Gaviard that we had dinner with back in late October, correct?" I asked.

"Yep, that's him. He reports to the French Chief of Defense, General Bentégeat, who, in turn, reports to the president, through the MOD. In times of crisis, however, General Bentégeat has a direct link to Chirac." He was, of course, referring to French President Jacques Chirac. *Well,* that *clears it up,* I thought.

"Now, Jeff," I said, somewhat thinking out loud, "how do I best get a meeting with the French Joint Staff J-3?" Meanwhile, I hoped that Gaviard had remembered me positively from that October dinner. "You don't think I pissed off any of those generals that night, do you?" I joked.

Pausing for a few seconds as if he was seriously contemplating my question, Colonel Jackson responded, "Well, as far as the brigadier generals went, I think you made a good impression, but I'm not sure about the three-star. Didn't you ask him, because of his last name, if he was related to a former Basque rebel?"

"Oh, duh, I forgot about that!" I said as we both laughed out loud. Of course, I hadn't asked Gaviard that, but by now Jeff and I knew each other well enough that we could chuckle over that kind of ribbing.

"Rick, I think the best person to start with is Major Kulmayer. He's our US liaison to the French Joint Staff for a reason, and as far as I can tell, he has good credibility and solid contacts with the French. As you know, we share a lot of operational information with the French, as they do with us," said Jackson.

"Jeff, if you see him, please ask him to stop by. In the meantime, I'll ask Becky Bouvier to contact him at the Joint Staff," I said.

In a surprisingly short ten minutes, Jackson returned . . . with Major Jeff Kulmayer, who shared Jackson's first name. Kulmayer had been in our office spaces talking to one of the Army attaché NCOs before heading back over to the French Joint Staff for the day.

"Sir, Colonel Jackson explained to me the overall situation, and I believe I can get in to see General Gaviard today, to set up an appointment between you and him," said Major Kulmayer. "If you give me a block of time that is best for you, like Tuesday afternoon, for example," he continued, "I'll take it from there. Gaviard actually seems like a pretty decent guy, so I don't expect any problems."

"Actually, Jeff, that time block sounds perfect. Tuesday afternoon would be great. Alternatively, since there is some urgency to this, I'll take Wednesday morning or Thursday morning as well," I said. "But it needs to happen this week."

"Roger that, sir," came the reply. "I'll do my best."

That night, at 5:45, fifteen minutes before the embassy's official closing, I heard a knock on my open doorframe. I looked up from my large, decades-old oak desk, and there was Jeff Kulmayer.

"Jeff, what do you have for me, sir?" I asked.

"Sir, General Gaviard can't see you tomorrow afternoon, but you're on for Wednesday morning, 0900, at his office. I suggest that I wait for you just inside the main gate off *Boulevard St. Germain*, and then I'll just escort you straight to his office. I'd say be there no later than 0845."

"Done deal, Jeff. I'll be there by 8:45."

"By the way," added Kulmayer, "General Gaviard wanted to know what the meeting was about, so I hope you don't mind . . . I gave him a heads-up that it had to do with US advance notification for US military aircraft to enter French air space. General Gaviard looked at me with a bit of a quizzical look, but didn't say anything else, so . . . I'm not quite sure what to expect," he concluded. "But like I said, he seems like a reasonable guy."

"Roger, Jeff," I replied. "We'll see what Wednesday brings. I hope I don't shoot my toe off trying to get this thing accomplished for whatever might be about to happen with Iraq."

Major Jeffrey Kulmayer chuckled and walked out of my office.

Left envisioning how this "negotiation" might go, I realized it wouldn't be a negotiation at all. I had been given exactly zero by the US Department of Defense in the way of something to negotiate *with*. What this was going to come down to, I realized, was nothing more than a request (heck, maybe even a plea, if I had to go there), from one long-standing military ally to another, and one from one military professional to another. *The fact that our political masters are not exactly getting along might complicate things,* I thought.

Either the French were going to say "*oui*" or "*non*." If they said "oui," it would come down to *how many* hours of advanced warning they would accept. Right now, it was twenty-four. In normal peacetime or Cold War conditions, that was probably reasonable. But for furthering the US buildup in the Middle East, or, for a far more challenging scenario, conducting combat operations in Iraq, shorter notification timelines were necessary for optimal operational flexibility. They would allow

US commanders and planners to meet rapidly emerging challenges and situations from their supporting headquarters in Europe. Getting this time restriction reduced was a big deal. But I was a bit concerned. *What the heck do I know? I am an Army officer,* I thought. *Planning global air transport operations is not my forte.*

As an Army artillery officer, however, I did know about—in fact, was quite competent at—coordinating and deconflicting air space within an Army division or corps operations area. But I knew next to nothing about US Air Force long-range fighter, bomber, or global transportation operations. *I certainly hope the conversation does not need to go there, or worse, get technical,* I thought.

In an effort to get conversant in this operational blind spot, I decided to sit down with Jackson to at least get the right terminology down before my discussion with Gaviard. I figured it was better to be over-prepared than under-prepared. On Tuesday afternoon, we spent a couple of hours talking about the overall subject. However, after a few minutes, it was clear Jackson's knowledge about global air transport operations was also somewhat limited. He did, however, as a fighter pilot, know the basics of crossing international airspace, and a quick primer about that was quite helpful.

As Wednesday morning, March 12, 2003, arrived and I headed for the embassy via the metro at 7:20 in the morning, I realized I was not nervous at all in advance of this consequential meeting at the French Joint Staff. *Should I be?* I asked myself.

For some reason, I was feeling exceptionally calm. I knew that if I came back empty-handed, or with only a slight reduction from the current twenty-four-hour notification time, I would have failed, at least on this first try. But that would not have been the end of it. I could then appeal to Ambassador Leach for help, if I had to. Or perhaps the US Air Force four-star general who had stopped at the embassy a few weeks prior could help. But that was essentially negative thinking, perhaps even presaging failure, so I put those thoughts out of my mind.

As it was nearing peak traffic time, my driver, Thierry, and I departed the embassy at 2 *rue Gabriel* for 231 *Boulevard St. Germain,* leaving ourselves plenty of time. On a normal day it would only take us no more than ten minutes to drive the simple route through the Place de la Concorde, over the Seine River on the *Pont de la Concorde* bridge and then taking a left turn onto *Boulevard St. Germain,* with the Joint Staff (and Army Staff) only another 400 meters or so farther on the right side. However, today we would allow for twenty minutes, because the traffic on *Boulevard St. Germain,* which ran parallel to the Seine on the left bank, was known for getting backed up fairly quickly. I called ahead to let Jeff know we were departing early, and he immediately came back with "Roger."

As Thierry and I pulled up to the arched drive-through at 231 *Boulevard St. Germain,* a French Army guard was there to meet us. Thierry discreetly placed a US embassy-provided pass above the dashboard, and the guard quickly let us through. It was apparent that Kulmayer had greased the skids with the French Security Office for our easy entry.

When I exited the vehicle, Jeff led me into a nearby alcove, where I had to surrender my French diplomatic ID card for a pass to be worn on the lapel of my uniform. Fortunately, I had already been in this rectangular building complex, which took up the better part of a city block, while visiting my contacts on the French Army Staff. Inside was a parking area that held about thirty-five cars, most of which I imagined belonged to either general officers or perhaps a few select colonels or civilians.

Kulmayer led the way, taking me straight to Gaviard's office. The building seemed at least seventy to eighty years old, although it was probably much older than that, with large oak doors, and in most places wooden plank floors covered with carpeting. Several offices had an outer room for a secretary, and through which a visitor had to pass, with the principal officer's larger office in the back.

As we went through the outer doors of Gaviard's office, we were greeted by an air force officer, roughly in his early thirties. Gaviard must have heard our voices because he presented himself to me within a few seconds, with a *"Bonjour, mon colonel, comment allez-vous?"*

"Très bien, mon general," I responded. *"Et vous, mon general?"*

Switching to English, he said, "Rick, I'm doing well. Would you like a coffee?"

"Sir, I would very much appreciate that," I responded.

His calling me by my first name this early in our conversation probably meant one of two things. A: He remembered my name from our dinner in October, or B: He had his secretary or military aide confirm it before I arrived. In either case, it made me more relaxed. However, I would address him as "sir" or "general."

After asking the secretary outside of his office to bring two coffees, he asked me to take a seat at the side of his desk, so the desk was not formally positioned between him and me.

"So, how is your new job going? I don't think you have been at it more than a week or so, have you?" he asked.

"No, sir, I have not," I replied. "It's been quite the whirlwind for the past several days." He laughed.

"I bet it has. Well, I am sure you will do just fine."

After briefly chatting with Gaviard about Dupré, for whom we both expressed admiration, the French airman brought us each *un café express*—an espresso-style coffee. As I drank it, it reminded me very much of the *espresso lungo* I drank with the Italian mountain troops: a tad watered-down and probably made with a small, portable, and steel espresso pot, the kind where you had to wait for the water to boil before it was ready.

"So," Lieutenant General Gaviard continued, "how can I help you?"

"Well, sir, I'm here to ask you about the notification time we— er, the American Air Forces—must provide, so that we may gain authorization to enter and cross your national airspace. As you know, it's currently—."

Gaviard cut me off, though politely. "I know, I know, it's twenty-four hours."

I again started to speak, saying, "Right, sir, but—"

Interrupting me yet again, he said, "Rick, I'll tell you what, six hours notification will be just fine, and if you need less than that for special situations, just let us know. Will that work?" he asked.

I was simultaneously dumbstruck and thrilled. *Six* hours? Down from twenty-four hours? Just like that? *Did he just say that*? And "Oh, by the way, if you need less time . . . *just ask us*." *Did he just say that too*?

After a brief pause, I said, "Sir, I am very, very grateful, and I think you know our Chairman of the Joint Chiefs, General Richard Myers, will be very grateful, as will our country."

Honestly, I didn't know if this issue had gotten to Myers' level, but I fully expected that it had, so in this case, I was sure as heck going to drop his name into the conversation.

"Rick, no problem," Gaviard said. "By the way, for being the token Army guy, it was good to have you and your wife at the Air Chief's dinner in October." He smiled kindly.

"Sir, I appreciated that you let a knuckle-dragging ground-pounder like me join you, as did my wife."

With that, I bid Lieutenant General Patrick Gaviard *au revoir*, and while leaving his office, I half-entertained *running* out, just on the off chance he might change his mind. As I met Kulmayer outside of the general's office, I gave him a thumbs-up and a big smile. He smiled back, knowing this was a very good day for both of us, not to mention for the US Armed Forces and the United States.

Gaviard would contact me, almost a year later, for assistance in expediting his son's US visa so that he could attend an internship in Washington D.C. One can well imagine how that request would jump to the top of my "to-do" list.

CHAPTER 15

WAR

ON TUESDAY, MARCH 18, 2003, ONE WEEK after the meeting with Lieutenant General Gaviard, I arrived at the US Embassy and headed up to my office. Upon arrival, I immediately accessed the Internet to see what might be new. There was, in fact, a lot new.

The previous evening, President Bush, in a nationally televised speech to the American people, essentially said war with Iraq was at hand. Not divulging the exact times nor location, he pointed to the next forty-eight hours for "liberating" Iraq from its tyrannical leader and Western thorn in the side, Saddam Hussein. No clear evidence of Iraqi WMD programs had been found, but now the US political pressure for war, accompanied by far fewer international allies than in 1991 Gulf War, was reaching a peak.

The day, while anxieties were certainly heightened among all US Embassy employees and families, was rather uneventful. When I returned the next morning on Wednesday, the 19th of March, that had changed. Early that morning, the US had initiated massive combat operations against the Iraqis from the air and sea. Images of buildings in Baghdad being hit with cruise missiles or combat aircraft-delivered bombs, along with eerily empty streets and the occasional taxi driving by, were repeatedly shown on the major international television news networks around the world. Ground-launched operations could not be far behind.

At the country team meeting, the ambassador asked I provide a brief overview of the situation, which I did, with only unclassified, "open source" information. The biggest concern locally, of course, was the safety of US family members, particularly as children went to school or as mothers and fathers were out and about taking care of family business. Our embassy regional security officer provided local threat information and additional security guidance.

Fortunately, we had practiced our embassy communications and contact network just a few weeks prior, and some of us were given special phones in the event French telephone coverage might be compromised. The ambassador also decided every bus carrying American children to school would have an onboard escort, at least for the next few weeks, or until an updated threat assessment could be made.

After weeks of international and US internal debate, including significantly different military force assessments between what US Army Chief of Staff General Erik Shinseki thought was required to successfully "liberate," and more importantly, stabilize Iraq after initial combat operations and what senior Defense Department officials thought was needed, the war was on. There was no turning back. In the following days, in an impressive display of military combined arms operations, US and coalition forces completely overwhelmed the Iraqi military.

But a few senior officers, myself included, were concerned about the "day after." Hearkening back to US involvement in the Balkan conflicts of the late 1990s, while attending Harvard's Kennedy School as a senior service college fellow, I remember talking to a former US Army division commander, Major General Bill Nash, who commanded the 1st Armored Division and led US ground forces, called Task Force Eagle, into northern Bosnia. Eagle's mission was to stabilize and secure Bosnia after the violence and destruction that had racked that Balkan country in the preceding three years.

Slightly paraphrasing, Major General Nash said, "When we crossed the Sava River and went into Bosnia from Croatia, I needed two things to effectively do my job: major air support—which I could recall at the snap of a finger and which would appear over my head in an instant, to show the warring factions that I had more than sufficient power to enforce the peace—and a huge bag of cash on the hood of my HMMWV."

Of course, Major General Nash did *not* enter Bosnia with a huge bag of cash on his HMMWV. His metaphorical point, however, was that after years of devastation (when I overflew Bosnia in 1997 in a CH-47 helicopter, some places looked like a moonscape, with some completely destroyed and empty villages), Bosnia would require much, much more than occupying military forces. It would cost hundreds of millions, if not billions, of US and international funds—and thousands of people—to rebuild. (To this day, Bosnia, while in far better shape than in the late 1990s, is still not completely stable, as ethnic, political, and religious differences continue to threaten it.)

By April 9th, 2003, US and coalition forces had reached Baghdad. Looting of government and public buildings, including museums and armories, was rampant in what appeared to be mass disorder. This was the first sign that perhaps Army Chief of Staff Shinseki, who had been the Army's Deputy Chief of Staff for Operations during the initial US ground operations in Bosnia and later commanded US Army, Europe (in which I served as a battalion commander) forces in 1997 in the Balkans, might have been right when he declared that the US would need roughly three times the forces on the ground now in Iraq to stabilize and secure the country. Senior Department of Defense officials, including Defense Secretary Donald Rumsfeld and Deputy Defense Secretary Paul Wolfowitz, dismissed General Shinseki's assertion. Wolfowitz called it "wildly off the mark."

CHAPTER 16

HEAD OF
THE LINE

THE POLISH EMBASSY IN PARIS has a special place in US military attaché lore. It was the scene of a chance—if not comical—yet momentous encounter between the then-US military attaché to France, Major General Vernon Walters, and the Chinese military attaché, Fang Weng. On April 27th, 1970, the date of the encounter, the United States and China did not yet have official diplomatic relations. Prior to this, Walters was prohibited from shaking hands, speaking with, or even acknowledging a Chinese diplomat's presence.

However, on this spring day in 1970, Walters was in possession of a letter personally given to him by Dr. Henry Kissinger, President Nixon's then-National Security Advisor and Bavarian-born future Secretary of State. Kissinger had become a naturalized US citizen through his service in the US Army during World War II and subsequently went on to a brilliant academic career at Harvard University. In essence, the letter, which Kissinger tasked Walters to present to the Chinese mission in Paris, said that the United States was prepared to hold secret talks concerning the war in Vietnam, if the Chinese desired them. These talks could be kept completely confidential, the letter indicated, and the president was prepared to send a high-level representative (Dr. Kissinger) to the Chinese communists in Paris to lead such talks for the United States.

Walters had just walked out of the reception held in the Polish embassy and ambassador's residence. He found himself in the embassy courtyard with the Chinese military attaché, one Fang Weng. There was nobody else present. Walking up to Weng, in French, Walters said, "I am Vernon Walters, and I have a message for your government from my president."

Walters described the encounter in his memoirs, *Silent Missions*, a few years later: "He looked at me, and his mouth dropped open. He tried to say something and he could hardly speak. Finally, he gasped in French, 'I'll tell them; I'll tell them; I'll tell them!' and jumped into his Mercedes-Benz and drove off."

It would take another three months before Walters could discreetly deliver the letter directly to the Chinese ambassador, at the ambassador's residence, a mansion located in the Paris suburb of Neuilly. At the time, all accredited diplomats had "CD" (*corps diplomatique* or diplomatic corps) license plates, numbered according to the countries they represented.

Moving around Paris, Walters often had to be completely discreet. He had to plan where to park and how far to walk to his intended location to lose any possible active surveillance, prying journalists, or just nosy passersby. The public discovery of high-level, US-Chinese government contacts in Paris, given that both countries did not have official diplomatic relations, would have made world news and required both governments to expend far more energy, not to mention political capital, in responding to the press and public than in holding the "talks" themselves. As such, the evening was often the best time for such a mission.

Walters' delivery mission to the Chinese ambassador was successful, with the Chinese ambassador complimenting the American general on his discreet approach.

Thus, the secret "Paris peace talks" with the Chinese were initiated in July 1970. The more public (and plodding) US peace talks with the North Vietnamese, led by US Ambassador-at-Large Averell Harriman, had already been ongoing for over a year. With the newly initiated and secret US-China talks, Walters began smuggling Kissinger, who would arrive via a French military airfield on the outskirts of Paris, into his Neuilly (a leafy Paris suburb) apartment. To hide Kissinger's identity, such as when Walters' housekeeper asked how to address the intermittent guest in his apartment, Walters would refer to Kissinger as "General Harold Kirschmann," believing the common first letters of each name would lower the risk of a slip-up.

On April 17th, 2003, at about 1930 hours, I arrived via *Rue Dominique* with Susan at the Polish Embassy and ambassador's residence for a reception held by the ambassador. As soon as we pulled up to the gate, an embassy guard arrived to open Susan's right rear door on the curbside, while another went around to open my street side door. As she stepped out of the car, I thought Susan looked stunning in her blue sequin evening gown. I was wearing Army blues with a white shirt and black four-in-hand knotted tie, typical for this type of official diplomatic event after 6:00 p.m. Walking across the large, packed-surface portico to the mansion's massive doors, we beheld an impressive structure, all the more so with the sun on a low horizon, brightly illuminating the building's upper half.

The Polish ambassador's mansion had an impressive history. In 1772 Princess Marie-Catherine de Brignole, having recently separated from her husband, Honoré III, Prince of Monaco, purchased one of the last available plots of land in the central Parisian district of Saint Germain. She then had a palace built that would portray her rank and social status to the French public, with the goal of making it grander and more elaborate than the nearby *Hôtel de Matignon* (currently home to France's Prime Minister).

Unfortunately for the princess, she did not take much pleasure in her new home and stayed in it only until 1790, when she emigrated to England. Since she had originally rented the palace to the British ambassador, the palace was seized by the revolutionary government and later passed through several owners, including the English banker William Williams-Hope, who owned it from the early to mid-1800s. Hope turned the palace into a sumptuous residence, expanding it greatly to include a second floor, a porter's lodge, a set of wings, and a significantly enlarged main body. The house was thereafter no longer viewed as a Parisian *hôtel*, but something much grander.

Hope died in 1855 and bequeathed all his earthly possessions, including the house to an English friend, who proceeded to sell everything. Again passing through several hands, the house was sold in 1936 to the Polish Ministry of Foreign Affairs as the Polish legation's permanent post in Paris. Since then it has continuously served as the home to the Polish ambassador and his staff, interrupted only for the duration of World War II, when it became a German cultural office.

By the time Susan and I crossed the portico and reached the palace's outer marble steps, we could see that a long line of reception guests had already formed, extending up the magnificent staircase with white marble columns at the top. There must have been at least fifty people ahead of us, waiting to go through the receiving line. As it turned out, that line was at the top of the steps and adjacent to a magnificent burgundy and white-marbled ballroom.

All of a sudden, standing before Susan and I was a thirtysomething Polish man in a dark blue business suit. He had just walked down the entire flight of white marble and burgundy-carpeted stairs, passing the waiting guests and walking right up to us before we even stood on the first step. Glancing at my nametag first, he looked me squarely in the eyes and said in very good English, "Colonel and Mrs. Steinke, please follow me!"

Without even giving us the chance to say "sure" or "my pleasure," the young man did an about-face and briskly led Susan and me up the staircase. Susan was wearing high heels, and I was afraid she was not going to be able to keep up, so I slowed the pace a bit, putting some distance between me and the young Polish man, who by now was practically bounding up the stairs. Figuring he probably *wanted* to get well ahead of me, I didn't worry about catching up to him. However, I was worried, sort of, about what all the ambassadors, generals, French government officials, and others were thinking as this forty-something American military attaché and his wife were bypassing the entire lot of them.

Arriving at the top of the steps, I turned around to make sure Susan was right behind me. In the back of my mind was the thought that the ambassador was going to say something about the excellent military operations we had just jointly conducted in Iraq. Roughly a week after Baghdad had fallen, while there were certainly ongoing security concerns, the initial military operations were a major success. The country-wide violence and signs of an insurgency would not begin until several weeks later, so an air of a victory celebration was still lingering.

Signaling to the next couple about to go through the receiving line that we were about to cut in front of them, the Polish protocol officer at the start of the receiving line announced my name and that of "Madame Steinke" to the Polish ambassador and his wife.

As I extended my hand to the ambassador, he said, "What a great agreement our two countries have reached! Poland very much looks forward to working closely with the United States on this excellent achievement!"

Agreement? What agreement? I thought. Not missing a beat, however, I reflexively responded with choice words.

"Mr. Ambassador," I began, "all the way back to the days of Colonel Kosciuszko and our Revolutionary War, Poland and the United States have been great friends and allies. We very much look forward to continuing our close partnership."

"Indeed, Colonel, indeed," he said, smiling broadly.

Susan and I then moved on to the nearby reception hall.

I had no clue as to what *agreement* the ambassador was talking about. I was also going to make darn sure he did not learn that fact. Nor would his defense attaché, Navy Captain Ireneusz Goreczny, learn about it. When I ran into the jovial Goreczny later in the evening, I brought up the Iraq war and European soccer, anything to keep him from talking about—or worse, *asking* about—this "agreement," about which I didn't have the slightest clue.

I threw Colonel Kosciuszko's name out to the ambassador because I knew something about Kosciuszko. I knew he was a Polish colonel, and that he had served with the Continental Army of the American Revolution. Was my knowledge of American military history that keen? No, it definitely was not.

However, I *did* remember his name because at West Point, just off "the Plain," the main parade ground, and right across the street by the Hudson River, there is a towering statue to Colonel Thaddeus Kosciuszko, whom all cadets learn about their first year at the Academy. Behind that statue was also a good place to take a date and hold his or her hand, or—God forbid—share a kiss (which, alas, I never did), beyond the prying eyes of Academy officers who prohibited such "personal displays of public affection," or PDA. It was not as good a place for that as West Point's Flirtation Walk, but it would certainly do. And that made it a hard-to-forget reference point.

As it turned out, the snap decision to throw Kosciuszko's name out there was not a bad call. Not only had he, much like General Lafayette from France, come to America in 1776 to join the revolution, the exceptionally competent and adventurous Polish engineer had received a colonel's commission in the Continental Army. After he performed superbly for the fledgling American Army over the next eight years, the Continental Congress voted to bestow him the rank of brigadier general in 1784. Brigadier General Kosciuszko then returned to Poland the same year, this time to fight for Polish freedom from Russian influence.

He would return to the US in 1796 for a short time, developing a close relationship with Thomas Jefferson. Kosciuszko died in

Switzerland in 1817. However—and I hoped this fact was most relevant to the Polish ambassador—Kosciuszko became a famous Polish national hero and is buried in Krakow, Poland, along with Polish Kings. It was pure dumb luck to remember his name in front of the ambassador.

Arriving back at my embassy office the next morning, I decided to briefly check the Internet for any new developments in Iraq. There, in a big headline from BBC News, was my answer to what "agreement" the ambassador was referring to: "Poland Buys US Fighter Jets," said the headline. Apparently, just hours before my arrival at the Polish ambassador's residence, our two countries had concluded a deal for the US sale of F-16s to Poland. The Polish defense minister called it "the contract of the century."

As an Army captain named Marco Lovell once told me, "There are times I'd rather be lucky than good." This was one of those times I was just plain lucky.

CHAPTER 17

FIRST BLOW

BEGINNING WITH FRENCH FOREIGN MINISTER Dominique Villepin's speech at the UN and continuing with French President Jacques Chirac's announcement that France would veto any UN vote for war against Iraq, by late April 2003 and into May, the discord between the US and French governments over the Iraq War began to reach a crescendo. In the United States, there were public demonstrations against France, with bottles of Bordeaux wine being poured down street drains and references to French "cheese-eating surrender monkeys" abounding seemingly everywhere, or so the US and international mass media portrayed.

Meanwhile, in Europe, there was beginning to be talk among the other anti-Iraq War countries, like Belgium and Germany, that perhaps France and other European countries should advocate for Europe's own defense organization, outside of NATO. In this same period, in remarks attributed to (although never acknowledged by) US national security advisor Condoleezza Rice, it was stated that the United States should "punish France, ignore Germany, and forgive Russia," with all three countries abstaining from any involvement in the Iraq War. As the month of May began, President Bush gave a speech on an American aircraft carrier, with a huge, not-so-subtle

"Mission Accomplished" banner in the background, extolling the American victory over the Iraqis.

The first signs of how the "punish France" policy would be implemented became evident in fairly short order. That punishment would be mainly felt—and directed toward—the French armed forces and the relationships those forces had with their US counterparts. While my fellow US attachés and I—along with many US diplomats in Paris—questioned the wisdom of that approach (since it was not the French military that decided not to deploy to Iraq, but rather, their political masters), it was our duty to implement the policy, and that we did . . . mostly, pushing back when I thought it right to do so.

The first stark indicator of "punish France" became clear to my DAO team and me on May 8th, 2003. On May 8th of each year in France there is a major national celebration commemorating the anniversary of World War II's V-E (Victory in Europe) Day. Traditionally, they hold ceremonies, make speeches, recognize veterans, award medals, and the like, somewhat akin to the American Memorial Day. The epicenter of these events in France is Paris's Arch of the Triumph, where the French president, prime minister, and minister of defense, among other French national leaders, are in attendance. For this particular commemoration the Arch of the Triumph is ringed with aluminum bleachers. Some of these bleachers will host French schoolchildren and local citizens, while others are reserved for the international diplomatic corps in Paris, mainly ambassadors and military attachés.

About three to four months before the 2003 V-E Day ceremonies, the US Marine Corps War College indicated it would be bringing a contingent of its students to Paris. Later hosting other war colleges (such as the National War College, which was an annual visitor to the embassy), I learned that this meant that about a dozen or so students in the ranks of lieutenant colonel and colonel, plus two or three faculty members, would be visiting from the Marine War College at Quantico, Virginia.

When French Army chief of staff General Bernard Thorette heard of the visit, he was ecstatic. Like General Bentégeat, General Thorette was a *troup de marine*, the French equivalent of a US Marine. Furthermore, General Thorette had commanded a regiment of French marines in Operation Daguet, the name given to the French military operation that participated in Operation Desert Storm, in 1991. This French Marine regiment, deploying adjacent to the US 82nd Airborne Division, would secure the left flank of the entire coalition ground operation.

As a French Marine, General Thorette was eligible to hold the French Army chief of staff position, thereby putting him in charge of all French ground forces. This is because French Marines are fully integrated into the French Army, unlike their US counterparts, who are part of the Department of the Navy.

General Thorette was very respected among French soldiers and the French people. A man of letters, he spoke fluent Arabic and some Spanish, as well as played the saxophone. I found him tall—often the tallest man in the room—but like his colleague and superior, General Henri Bentégeat, calmly confident, never arrogant, and always approachable.

I arrived at the Arch of the Triumph at 9:45 in the morning on May 8th, 2003, with an official guest as well as a personal friend, Major General Brian Tarbet, the commander of the Utah Army national guard. I was immediately approached by General Thorette's military aide-de-camp, Major Olivier Lardans. I had spoken to Lardans, a very friendly and helpful officer, a few times in the past, so we knew each other in advance of this encounter.

"Good morning, sir," began Lardans.

"Good morning, Olivier," I replied.

"I just want to confirm that the Marine War College visit is still on."

The Marine Corps War College visit was to happen in under two weeks. Having just spoken with my DAO teammate and Marine

Corps attaché, Lieutenant Colonel William "Buzz" Holdorf, about the matter at our Monday morning attaché meeting, I assured him it was.

"Indeed, it is, Olivier," I confirmed. "No worries."

"Sir, that is great. General Thorette really wants to roll out the red carpet for them. He has over 100 French and international guests confirmed for the reception," he said. "And, of course, the French Army Band will be there as well."

"That's great. I'm sure it will be awesome and very much appreciated by our American Marines," I replied.

Major Lardans then walked down the bleacher steps to take his spot not far from France's second-highest ranking Marine and the leader of the French Army.

As I thought about what the major had just said, I imagined it would be quite the impressive affair. The residence of the French Army Chief of Staff is in *Les Invalides*, the historical, prominent, and massive multi-storied stone structure located just south of the Alexander III bridge. To its front is a spacious green esplanade about the size of a couple of American football fields, greeting visitors before they reach the arched entryway leading to *Les Invalides'* cobblestone courtyard, at least as big as a football field in terms of square meters.

Les Invalides was built in the late 1600s by Louis XIV, France's Sun King, for the invalids of France's wars. French veterans still reside there. *Les Invalides* is also home to a magnificent, gold-domed chapel, as well as an impressive French military museum and Napoleon Bonaparte's tomb. Inside the structure, the large courtyard is used for ceremonies such as military funerals, a place for bestowing medals upon active French soldiers, as well as veterans, French and international alike.

Within no more than five minutes of Lardans walking away, Lieutenant Colonel Holdorf walked up to me, his face slightly pale.

"Sir, you are not going to believe this," he said. "This morning I went by the office, and there was a fax from the Marine Corps War College."

"And . . . ?" I asked.

"They are not coming. The Marine War College visit is off," he stated.

"*What*? What do you mean it's *off*?"

"They are not coming. They said they are going elsewhere," he replied.

"Going *elsewhere*? Why? What the hell does *that mean*?" I asked.

"I'm not exactly sure. I just know they are not coming to Paris."

"Well, I just told the general's aide, maybe five minutes ago, that they *are* coming, and I expect by now General Thorette has gotten that word," I said.

Knowing that bad news does not get better with age, I told Holdorf, "We have to deliver this news to General Thorette *now*, before the ceremony starts, which it will in about six or seven minutes." Then, making what I'm sure Holdorf thought was an obvious statement, with a pit in my stomach, I said, "He's going to like hearing this about as much as getting a root canal."

As Holdorf and I made our way down the aluminum bleacher steps through the ever-thickening crowd of ambassadors, diplomats, and military attachés, we had maybe fifteen feet to go before reaching France's Army Chief of Staff. Looking to my left, I saw Major Lardans. As our eyes locked, I shook my head. In the next instant I turned my head, not waiting to see his expression in response.

We approached Thorette, who was standing on the pavement in front of the first bleacher row, while facing the Arch of the Triumph, from behind. With the ceremony's start now just a few minutes away, people in the crowd were still conversing, which meant that most bystanders would fortunately not hear the disappointing news we were about to deliver, nor be able to observe the response. It was small consolation that this was not going to be more of a spectacle.

Stepping slightly around his right side and in front of him as we moved into his field of view, Thorette turned slightly and looked at both of us.

Facing the general, who looked at us with his normally positive countenance, Holdorf hesitated a second, and then began: "*Mon general*, I am very sorry to inform you the Marine Corps War College is not coming to Paris as we had thought just a few days ago. They have had a change of plans."

Switching his eyes from Holdorf, Thorette, his facial expression now completely changed, shot a glance at me.

"They are *not coming*?" he asked.

"No, sir," I said. "We are sorry, but they have had to change their plans."

After what was probably five seconds but seemed ten times longer than that, the now red-faced and shaking general said, "Well, I am *very* sorry to hear that." And then he turned his back to us.

It was if we had just told Thorette that someone had poisoned his dog.

As the general did not want to hear another word at this point, Holdorf and I headed back up to our spot in the bleachers with the other international military attachés.

With the Arch of the Triumph my focal point as the V-E Day commemoration ceremony began, I thought, *If the intent here was to insult the French Army chief of staff, whoever suggested this slap in the face was mighty damn successful.* I further pondered at what level this idea might have been hatched, and who ultimately made the decision to do it. Knowing US Marine officers, I thought there was no way on God's green Earth a Marine officer had made this decision. At some level, I thought, it had to have been a civilian.

CHAPTER 18

PUNISHMENT
WITH LIMITS

ANOTHER INDICATOR OF THE "PUNISH France" approach and imposed changes to US-France military-to-military relations came a few days later as a directive from the Pentagon. It limited the participation of US military brass at the upcoming Paris Air Show, to be held in mid-June. The Paris Air Show is a massive bi-annual international aviation fair. Along with its sister UK airshow, the Farnborough Air Show (held in Paris in alternating years), it can be considered the mother of all aviation expos and trade shows. Huge commercial aviation and military deals, some of which are developed in advance of the show, are often signed at the event. For 2003, the Pentagon-based directive declared that no US military brass above the rank of 0-6 (colonel or Navy captain) would attend.

Overall lower US attendance at the 2003 Paris Air Show, which was held from the 15th to the 22nd of June, was yet another result of the bitter trans-Atlantic political dispute resulting from France's (and Germany's) opposition to the US-led Iraq War and the US's "punish France" policy. For the 2003 Air Show, word had been put out, either proactively or passively, concerning the Pentagon's approach. The presence of US commercial vendors was accordingly reduced, significantly so, to roughly 180 exhibitors at the show, versus roughly 350 just two years before. In the end, no US military officers above the ranks of colonel or Navy captain attended. There were also significantly fewer US congressional and government delegations.

As it turned out, the lack of high-ranking military officers and congressional delegations made my job easier. While the US Embassy Office of Defense Cooperation was the embassy's lead military office for the event, additional support for the event would have fallen on my military attaché team, along with other US embassy offices, such as the protocol, public affairs, and economics sections. While there was a lot of discussion surrounding the degree to which the United States might have lost business, no comprehensive nor conclusive study was ever done to verify this. To be fair, some big deals for aircraft purchases were still made with Boeing and its main European competitor, Airbus. Nonetheless, it was just another indicator of where the Bush Administration stood concerning France in 2003. It was becoming increasingly clear that "punish France" was not just for a day—it was a policy.

Meanwhile, another "punish France" measure arrived that I thought we were going too far in employing. This one came from our National Defense University at Fort McNair, Washington D.C. Again, I did not know at which Pentagon level each measure was decided or being managed. I suspected Rumsfeld, who was alleged to have managed by one-page and often one-line memos directed at subordinates for answers or action, simply told senior Pentagon generals and staffers to find ways to implement the "punish France" policy, and subordinates took it upon themselves to suggest the means. But I could never be sure.

Each year, and for many consecutive years, the French had received at least one slot to the National War College, a one-year in-resident master's degree level of study representing the pinnacle of professional military education (PME) for officers of all the US services. Also referred to as a "senior service college," this in-resident, year-long course of study is afforded to roughly the top ten to fifteen percent or so of the lieutenant colonels, colonels, Navy commanders, and captains of the US Armed Forces. For the 2003-2004 academic year the US National Defense University informed my DAO that the French would not receive a slot.

As it turned out, the French nominee for the 2003-2004 National War College academic year was to be an Army lieutenant colonel. But he wasn't just any French Army lieutenant colonel. He was the military aide to French President Jacques Chirac. Again, I'm not sure if this was known by the National Defense University at the time. I expect it was, however, as the notification came very late in the nomination and acceptance process. I visualized some DoD bureaucrat, at some level, thinking, *Hey, the French are going to nominate Jacques Chirac's military aide. This is our chance to stick it to 'em!* But again, I can't confirm that as fact.

I strongly believed not only in the international goodwill created by hosting international cadets at our service academies, military training schools, and senior service education institutions, but in the broadening experiences that *US officers* also received from their exposure to and interaction with these international officers. In my first year in Paris I was sought out by three (there would later be two more) international defense attachés assigned to Paris, each enthusiastically complimenting the American hospitality they had received, as well as the enriching experience they had while attending US military senior service colleges in the United States. Two of them, a Jordanian Air Force brigadier general and Moroccan Army colonel, were particularly memorable. Each extolled not only the hospitality they personally felt at the US Air War College and Army War College, respectively, but the warm welcomes their family members had received as well.

The Jordanian general, a practicing Muslim, was exceptionally effusive about his experience. Inviting Susan and me into his home in Paris to meet his family, he explained that what was most impressive was not the warm reception he personally received at the Air War College, but it was the way the college and *local citizens* of Montgomery, Alabama, teamed up to make his *family* feel welcome. Subsequent to his American experience, the Jordanian general said it was his dream to somehow find a way—and afford—to send his daughter for a master's degree in the United States.

In each senior service college annual class there are dozens of international officers. Course attendees are there to learn about strategy, leadership, logistics, international relations, and other warfighting and international security topics. It seemed to me, through the cultural exposure and enriching experience from being with a range of international officers, they learned a lot more than that.

Many of the international officers sent to US senior service colleges would also rise to very high rank, and it was in our interests to develop strong contacts with them as they ascended to positions of ever-increasing responsibility within their own countries. I previously pointed out the three French generals who each had US military educational experiences.

In view of the French receiving no slot to the National War College for 2003-2004, I decided to take it up with Ambassador Howard Leach. I knew it was not exactly a career-enhancing move to swim against the Washington tide of disdain for the French, but I thought this recent move was going too far. Targeting the French *military* for a decision they did not make, to stay out of the Iraq War, was the wrong response against the wrong target. As noted previously, the French armed forces were indeed training and fully preparing to deploy troops to Iraq. And these were not going to be token deployments, as was the case for many countries, who would send less than 100 people just so they could say they showed up and be on some list with their country flag. Depending on which troop deployment option they would have selected from those being considered in January 2003, the French would have been among the top five military forces in theater. But here we were, taking out our vitriol on French forces for a purely political decision.

The US response misread the Western concept of civilian control or oversight of the military, which is as strongly institutionalized in France as in other Western democracies. From every local indicator I had, the French military did not advise against intervention in Iraq. But even *if* they did, in the end, it was a civilian and political decision. And for the sovereign French government, was it the wrong one, given that roughly *eighty percent* of the French population was against a war with Iraq?

It was certainly not my intent to undermine overall US policy. However, I believed the US Army, Department of Defense, and government had not sent me to France to be a potted plant. Where I thought something against our national interests, I believed I was duty-bound to speak up. And I did. I decided to bring this specific case to Leach's attention.

I first engaged his executive assistant, Brandy Lowe. She had been working for the ambassador for several years as his chief scheduler, gate keeper, and confidant. She had followed him to Paris. Now she helped me schedule an appointment with the ambassador. The next day I appeared in front of her desk, posted just outside the ambassador's sumptuously paneled—with fireplace—office. Arriving a couple of minutes before our scheduled 3:00 p.m. meeting, I had given her a "heads-up" as to the meeting's topic.

"Good afternoon, Rick," she said. "Go right on in. Howard is waiting for you."

After exchanging some pleasantries with Leach, standing in front of his desk, I handed him the official message from the US National Defense University denying a French officer slot to the US National War College for the Academic Year 2003-2004. He silently read it.

After I saw he had finished, I interjected, "Mr. Ambassador, I think you should know this year's French nominee to attend the US National War College is President Chirac's personal military aide."

After pondering that statement for a few seconds, Leach looked up and said, "What? Really? That is absurd."

After the passing of several more seconds, Ambassador Leach continued: "This is quite petty, and taking the long view, it is not in our US national interests to deny a rising French military officer a slot."

"That is what I thought, too, sir," I replied. "But I also thought I would check with you before taking any action at my level."

"Rick," he responded, "I appreciate it. When I arrived here a couple of years back, I did not think we'd be dealing with something like this, especially after the tremendous sympathy we received from the French after the 9/11 attacks."

Ambassador Leach then picked up his phone and, rather than raise his voice to address Lowe, who was right outside his door, he said, "Brandy, please get Deputy Secretary Wolfowitz on the line for me."

It was almost 3:10 p.m. in Paris and 9:10 a.m., in Washington, D.C., so I wondered how much success Lowe would have tracking down "DEPSECDEF" Paul Wolfowitz at this hour. Was he in a meeting? Was he traveling, perhaps?

"Rick, sit down and relax," said the ambassador. "I'd like you to be here for this call, just in case I need to ask you something."

"Sure thing, sir," I responded, taking a seat in the chair in front of but slightly off to the left of the ambassador's antique desk.

As we began to talk about the spate of Americans pouring Bordeaux wine (which the ambassador liked but not to the degree he *loved* California wine) down America's street drains, his phone rang.

Picking up the receiver, he got Brandy Lowe, whom I could also half-hear through the office door: "I've got Deputy Secretary Wolfowowitz on the line," she said.

I was impressed that it had taken her less than five minutes to track down the number-two man in the Pentagon.

"Good afternoon . . . or rather, good morning to you, Paul," began the ambassador.

After a short listening pause, he continued, "Paul, we received a message from the National Defense University a couple of days ago, denying the French military a slot at the National War College this fall. Not that it matters *that* much, but the French's nomination for this year happens to be Jacques Chirac's military aide."

After another brief pause, with Leach listening to Deputy Secretary Wolfowitz, he continued, "But, Paul, is this what we *really* want to be about? To deny the French military and this rising officer an opportunity to attend our National War College, and moreover, deny our US officers a chance to interact with him? This comes across as *really petty*, don't you think?"

At this point, Leach listened again, but the rest of the conversation did not last long. Hanging up the phone, he said, "Rick, don't give this another thought. The French will get their National War College slot."

Hearkening back to my first day in the embassy, when I pondered who Howard Leach was and how his tour might go, and what it might be like be to work for him, I now had my first and clearest indicator. At that moment, I was darn proud to call him my boss. As we worked our way into and through the summer of 2003, I realized that, while he was a political appointee (and not a career US foreign service officer), as almost all US ambassadors in Paris were, his instincts for doing what was best for America were, in my humble opinion, spot-on.

I believed we were very fortunate to have him leading the US mission to France, particularly flying through the political flack of the day.

I also thought that though our current-day political flack was troubling, it was nothing compared to piloting (and parachuting) through the flak endured by the Greatest Generation and over the shores of Normandy. Little did I know that I would soon have the privilege to pay personal and physical tribute to those heroic Greatest Generation acts of sacrifice and service.

CHAPTER 19

PARACHUTE JUMP

THE MORNING OF MAY 12TH, 2003, BEGAN rather slowly as I worked my way through some emails from the Pentagon and the US State Department. The Pentagon emails were asking about the various bilateral-military programs we had with the French. *I am not looking forward to answering all of these probing questions,* I thought.

My pensiveness was then interrupted by our two DAO Army operations sergeants, Sergeant First Class Ralph Weld and Sergeant First Class Erik Math, who had just joined our team a few weeks prior.

Math had completed the US Army's Ranger School and wore the US Army RANGER tab, which we had in common. Now he stuck his head through my office door and, with a wide grin, said, "Hey, sir, how would you like to jump with us at Normandy this year?"

"Normandy? *Really?* Who is *'us?'*" I asked.

"Well, right now it looks like a company from the 82nd Airborne Division . . . and SFC Weld!" At this point, Weld entered through the doorframe where Math was standing and stumbled a bit.

"Hope your PLF is cleaner than that move," I joked to the Sergeant First Class. *PLF* stood for *parachute landing fall.*

Smirking at Weld, Math added, "Since it's an off year, a platoon or two is probably all they are going to send over here, but hey, Sergeant Weld and I think it would be pretty great! Whatdya think, sir?"

Not wanting to throw water on their exuberance, I said, "Sounds great to me! Let me check with 'big Army.' If they will let me throw my tired old ass out of a C-130, I'd be thrilled to do it with you guys!"

"Hoooahh!" replied Weld, and out the door they went.

What did I just do? I thought. *I haven't jumped out of a flying object and looked under a parachute canopy since 1991. What the heck am I thinking?*

Some twelve years earlier, in early April 1991, I had made two helicopter jumps, as well as one from a G-222, the Italian equivalent to the US Air Force's workhorse C-130 Hercules, a four-engine turboprop cargo and troop carrier. The three parachute jumps were in Italy's Dolomite Mountains, where, along with Italian alpine ("Alpini") paratroopers from nearby Bolzano, I landed on a still snow-covered, high-altitude meadow near the Italian village of *Alpe dei Siusi.*

On the day I jumped with the Italians, I was supposed to have been joined by American paratroopers from Vicenza, Italy. (At the time the US Army battalion-plus airborne infantry task force stationed there was commanded by Lieutenant Colonel John Abizaid, who went on to Command US Central Command during Operation Iraqi Freedom.) However, just the day prior they had been deployed to participate in Operation Provide Comfort, a NATO operation conducted along the Turkey-Iraq border intended to protect the Kurds from the still-lethal Saddam Hussein. Truth be told, I would have much preferred to have been with the Vicenza-based American paratroopers in Operation Provide Comfort, but such was the timing of my assignment with the Italian Alpini.

A parachute jump in Normandy, however, would be something truly extraordinary for any soldier. Prior to June 6, 1944, the pastoral and forested French coastal region called Normandy was little known to the world. On the morning of June 5, General Dwight D. Eisenhower gave the go-ahead for Operation Overlord, telling his troops, "You are about to embark upon the Great Crusade, toward which we have striven these many months. The eyes of the world are upon you."

On June 6, the Allies launched one of the largest amphibious invasions in history, with over 156,000 US, British, Canadian, Belgian, French, Dutch, Norwegian, New Zealand, Czech, and Greek troops carried across the English Channel by more than 5,000 ships. Normandy would forever become synonymous with sacrifice and heroism, and the great military and societal cause, which ultimately led to victory over Nazi Germany on May 8, 1945.

To this day, any visitor to the Normandy coast will witness the immense goodwill of Normandy's inhabitants to her liberators, with US, British, and Canadian flags prominently displayed on Normandy's church towers, schools, municipalities, and private balconies. Every year, on June 5 and 6, ceremonies and celebrations are held up and down the Normandy coast. US World War II veterans also return, often brought by their children or grandchildren, to the hallowed ground where they risked it all answering freedom's call. Often, platoons and companies of paratroopers from the active Army's storied 82nd Airborne Division or the 75th Ranger Regiment will also return to Normandy to commemorate the early-morning June 6 parachute drops by the two US airborne divisions, the 82nd and 101st divisions, minus the darkness, equipment, chaos, and combat.

Thinking further about Math and Weld's invitation, I realized it would be a tremendous honor and adventure. Sure, it had been a while since I had last jumped, and I had only made ten jumps in my Army career. But I didn't think an eleventh jump would be that big of a deal. Not being on official "jump status," meaning a soldier officially serving in a bona fide "airborne" position that required paratrooper training, I had to get special authorization, called "permissive jump status," from the Army Staff in the Pentagon. Fortunately, after about two weeks of waiting, that permission was granted, and I was cleared to jump at Normandy.

CHAPTER 20

GOOD DAY AT SAINTE-MÈRE-ÉGLISE

JUST TWO DAYS AFTER MENTIONING the prospect of jumping into Normandy, SFC Math again came to my office and announced, "Sir, they are not coming. The 82nd is not coming."

"What do you mean, they're *not coming*?"

"That's all I really know, sir," he replied, adding, "but I've been talking with some Special Forces contacts in Stuttgart, and it looks like SOCEUR is going to send some Army Special Forces to make the jump. I should know for sure in another day or so," he concluded.

I couldn't confirm if this cancellation was another "punish France" move by the DoD or if more important operational matters played a role in diverting the 82nd. Nonetheless, they were not coming to Normandy. But the Army "Green Berets" of the Special Operations Command, Europe (SOCEUR) . . . they might be making an appearance.

Math returned later that afternoon, a day before I thought he would deliver the final word, with the good news: "It's *on*, sir! SOCEUR has gotten US Air Forces Europe to commit an aircraft to supporting a jump at St. Maire Eglise!"

"That should be some real fun!" I replied.

June 5 finally arrived, and instead of driving up the night before, I decided to leave at 7:00 a.m. to make the ninety-minute drive from Paris to the French Air Force base at Evreux. Evreux is where we had planned a link-up with the Army Special Operations Forces from Stuttgart, Germany, before taking off in a C-130 to make our parachute drop a couple of miles outside of *Sainte-Mère-Église*.

Arriving at that morning, Weld, Math, and I found the French Air Force hangar where we were to meet our fellow parachutists. Pulling up to an old hangar that had apparently not seen much recent use, the two Army sergeants moved out ahead of me to see what the next steps were. Talking with some senior sergeants, we were directed to an area outside of the hangar with a couple of makeshift, three-feet-high wooden platforms for us to jump off, for simulating the most critical point of the jump: the landing.

The second aspect of jumping out of the plane was also reviewed for us by an Army Master Sergeant and "jumpmaster," who was certified in how to make sure a "stick"—or row of jumpers lined up on one side of the aircraft—knew all of the commands and procedures to safely exit the aircraft over a "drop zone."

Fortunately, before every jump, there is a review of the proper procedures for things like final equipment checks in the aircraft, hooking up to the static line, exiting the aircraft, checking your parachute once it deploys, deploying your reserve (in an emergency), avoiding other jumpers in the air, and landing. While I had made ten jumps before this Normandy jump, I paid very close attention to this refresher training, which lasted less than ninety minutes. Without it, I would have been a bit anxious. With it, and with both sergeants making sure all of my equipment was in good shape and reminding me of certain procedures, I was ready.

The only thing our parachute jump would approximate from the heroic jumps the intrepid soldiers of the 82nd and 101st Airborne Divisions made in the dark, early-morning hours of June 6th, 1944, was the location of where we would drop. Everything else would be different. Loaded down with weapons, ammunition, water, rations, and equipment, many of the 82nd "All American" and 101st "Screaming Eagle" paratroopers had been carrying fifty to sixty pounds of additional gear, barely able to shuffle onto the packed airborne vessels that would carry them across the English Channel. Instead, ours would be a "Hollywood" jump, with our main and reserve parachutes our only concerns and only additional weight.

Once we picked up, fitted, and checked each other's parachutes, we sat on the tarmac for almost an hour before boarding our designated C-130 from its gaping entry point at the back of the fuselage. As I was the senior officer in the group, I was among the first to enter the aircraft . . . and would be the first to exit.

We finally lifted off the Evreux airfield, heading north by northwest toward the English Channel, about thirty minutes before our designated drop time over a big cow pasture located about two miles outside of *Sainte-Mère-Église*. Not long after, my two fellow paratroopers and I realized that this was going to be a pretty rough ride.

"Hell, sir," said Math. "At least there is one aspect that comes close to the actual drop in 1944: this sucker is really bumpy." His face was becoming paler with each passing moment. To keep our minds off our flipping stomachs, we engaged in a bit of mindless banter.

"So, do you think they've changed our parachutes since 1944?" Weld asked. "Because right now, this airplane feels less advanced than the gliders that landed here almost sixty years ago!"

"Ha, I'll betcha these freakin' Air Force pilots *look* for turbulent air just to see if they can make us Army guys puke," said Math, adding, "but that *ain't gonna happen*."

After turning back from the sea and flying over the Normandy cliffs of Pointe-du-Hoc, I was thrilled to know we would soon be exiting the C-130. It was the worst turbulence I had experienced on any flight, military or civilian—ever. Thankfully, I hadn't eaten anything in about five hours. Had I done so, I might have embarrassingly "blown my cookies" in front of those great soldiers.

The rhythmic words of the US Army's "Jump School," many years before, kept easing themselves into my thoughts: *"Stand up, hook up, shuffle to the door."* They were the words that all American paratroopers sang about during long runs at dawn's first light, and remembered to their core. The jumpmaster finally signaled for us to stand up, hook up our static lines, recheck our static lines, and recheck our equipment. Once that was done, he motioned for me to position myself by the open door, with the French countryside zooming by below. Shuffling toward him, I slid my static line to him with my left hand until I was sure we both had a grip on it. I then made a ninety-degree turn toward the door, placing my right hand on the side of my reserve parachute, with my left foot placed slightly in front of my right.

As the jump caution light by the door turned *green*, the jumpmaster yelled, "Go!" and I did not hesitate, placing my left hand on the side of my reserve, with both hands now firmly pressing my reserve parachute from its sides, and immediately jumped up and out, while tucking my head down. I then counted: "One-one thousand, two-one thousand, three-one thou—" at which point I abruptly felt the opening shock and tug of my parachute. *Check canopy!* was the next "command" that entered my elated brain. Looking up, I saw a beautiful, olive green and fully opened silk canopy, with all parachute risers soon symmetrical and appropriately spaced. Looking straight down over the tips of my boots produced another reaction, however.

"Oh, *crap* . . . trees," I muttered.

I had been put out of the aircraft right over the top of a forest. The timing for when the pilot turns the jump caution light green is more art than science, involving a calculation of wind speeds, speed of the aircraft, and reaction times of the jumpmaster and jumpers. Approaching the edge of the drop zone, if the jump caution light goes green too early, jumpers can be endangered by exiting the aircraft over obstacles such as buildings, fences, trees, power lines, or bodies of water. If it comes on too late, not everyone may get out on a single pass over the drop zone, requiring perhaps a second, or even third, pass. The same issue of obstacles is true at the opposite end of a drop zone. Turn the green light off too late and you could again put soldiers out of the aircraft over or near dangerous obstacles.

For obvious reasons, trees present a danger to every paratrooper. Within an instant of seeing the trees below my dangling boots, I pulled on both toggles simultaneously as hard as I could, achieving forward lateral movement and steering the chute away from the tree line below me and toward the open pasture. Immediately upon clearing the trees, I noticed problems number two and three: a small creek and a fence. I wanted to avoid both, but given the rate I was dropping and the wind speed on the ground, I opted for risking a landing in the creek. My gamble would pay off, but just barely.

As I was about to land, now perhaps thirty-five feet above the ground, my lateral movement was parallel to and right over the top of the creek. I could not have aligned myself over the creek any better if I had tried (which I hadn't). I tried to gently pull my risers, but the rate of descent and forward movement were too much to try and make a last-minute steering correction. I would land in the corner of a fenced area, with fence about ten yards to my right and about fifteen yards in front of me, crossing from left to right. Meanwhile, unless a last-minute ground breeze hit me from the side, I was going to land in the creek.

Thoughts came in fractional seconds. *There is no way I can do a proper PLF,* I thought.

I hadn't been able to judge the creek's depth before, but I now thought it to be perhaps no more than one or two feet deep. If I had my legs pointed straight down, they could get stuck in the mud and then broken from the wind speed's forward momentum. So I made a split-second decision: to sit down, with my legs straight out. I landed with a soft but muddy *splat,* instantly realizing—and very thankful— that I was somehow uninjured. It turned out the creek was more of a muddy trough than a stream, with a trace of cow manure in it as well.

I smiled a premature smile, not knowing that the cow manure

was about to hit the fan. A gust of wind immediately grabbed my chute, jerking me forward and out of my seated position. I now found myself dragged facedown on my stomach toward the very fence, that third obstacle, I had been trying to avoid. Even as I reached the chest-high parachute release mechanism, I was jerked *through* the fence, with the fence's middle strand of steel wire snapping across my Kevlar helmet and shoulder. The force was so strong it pulled one of the fence's adjacent, four-foot wooden poles out of the soft mud. In the next instant, I pulled the tab, and my chute was finally released. Embarrassed but with only a bruise on my right shoulder, I slowly got to my knees and stood up.

"*Damn,* sir!" a soldier yelled, running to me from perhaps fifty feet away. "Are you okay?"

"I'm fine!" I replied, chuckling. "Although that fence *just about* kicked my ass!"

I wasn't sure how much the soldier had seen, but he'd obviously seen enough. I was covered in mud—with a slight cow manure effervescence—up to my waist. We had a pretty good laugh together (I must have made a helluva mud- and manure-covered sight), and I imagined he had a pretty good story to tell his fellow Green Berets that night.

Gathering up our parachutes, we headed off the drop zone, hearing the distant chatter of what must have been several hundred local French citizens who had been watching our airborne landing from a few small buildings and a copse of trees about 300 yards away. I was happy that my comical scene had been too far from their field of vision—or so I wanted to believe—for them to have fully observed my "unorthodox" landing. The Sainte-Mère-Église townspeople and other folks who were there treated us like heroes as we approached them, clapping, patting our backs, shaking our hands, and even giving the occasional hug. As I was a muddy, manure-smelling mess, I didn't get too many hugs. But I didn't care, as I was happy just to be walking off the drop zone under my own power.

The French people of the town of Sainte-Mère-Église treat American soldiers with great respect and admiration, some even as family. Each French family also adopts a couple of graves at the nearby American military cemetery above Omaha Beach, making sure that on Sundays and holidays they are adorned with flowers and they always—or so it's said—remember those soldiers in their prayers. After the jump, there was a small ceremony near a statue dedicated to the American liberators of Sainte-Mère-Église, and I was very happy that Susan, Erika, and Maria were able to join me for that post-jump event.

As I attended the large country team meeting the next week in the embassy, about twenty-five of my embassy teammates were present. Leach, who sat exactly opposite me at the large meeting table, asked, "So, Rick, I heard you made a parachute jump at *Sainte-Mère-Église* last week?"

"I did, sir," I responded.

"How did it go?"

"Mr. Ambassador," I responded, "any day you can *walk* away from a drop zone is a good day."

I thought of the intrepid paratroopers who landed and survived on D-Day, and smiled.

Our first photo in Paris, with Maria (L) and Erika (Steinke family photo)

Susan and I with General Bernard Thorette, in France's National Military Museum (Courtesy of the French Army Staff)

Susan and I with Major General (Select) Felix and Lin Dupre (Steinke family photo).

Meuse-Argonne Cemetery Superintendent Phil Rivers explaining the history of the cemetery. (Steinke family photo).

Maria with U.S. Ambassador Howard Leach and his dog Barkley, at the U.S. Ambassador's Residence (Steinke family photo)

With U.S. Naval Attaché, Captain Deak Childress and his wife, Mary Sue (Steinke family photo)

Meeting the Nigerian Defense Attaché, Major General Osita Chukwunedo Obierika (Courtesy Nigerian Embassy to France)

Performing my honored duty to annually change the flag over the Marquis de Lafayette's tomb at Picpus Cemetery, Paris (Courtesy U.S. Embassy Paris)

Smiling through the turbulence, Sainte-Mère-Église parachute
jump, with (L-R) SFC Erik Math and SFC Ralph Weld
(Steinke family photo)

Thanksgiving lunch with U.S. and international ladies
(Steinke family photo)

With Erika and Maria after the parachute jump at Sainte-Mère-Église (Steinke family photo)

Receiving a memento from French Minister of Defense Michèle Alliot-Marie after returning from the NATO summit in Colorado Springs, October 2003. (Courtesy French Ministry of Defense)

Greeting French Minister of Defense Michèle Alliot-Marie at Les Invalides, June 5, 2004 (Courtesy French Ministry of Defense)

Tom Hanks and Stephen Spielberg keeping a low profile at the 60th Anniversary of D-Day ceremonies, 6 June, 2004 (Courtesy Thierry Delavaud)

*President George W. Bush and President Jacques Chirac walking
"the bridge" towards the podium and awaiting D-Day veterans.
(Courtesy U.S. Embassy Paris)*

*(L-R) Greek Naval Attaché, Commander Jean Pavlopoulos; Susan;
Guri and Colonel John Hynaas, Norwegian Defense Attaché
at the annual Attaché Ball (Steinke family photo)*

Susan and Pierre Cardin, Theoule-sur-Mer (Steinke family photo)

*Pierre Cardin signing autographs for French and
U.S. Naval Officers (Steinke family photo)*

Delivering a speech at Theoule-sur-Mer's commemoration of the
Provence Landings and liberation by American soldiers
(Steinke family photo)

Laying a wreath at the WW II memorial near the town of
Theoule-sur-Mer (Courtesy Mayor's Office, Theoule-sur-Mer)

With Secretary of State Colin Powell at U.S. Embassy Paris.
As General Powell noted, "Maria wanted nothing to do with
this photo!" (Steinke family photo)

A divine discovery: the
U.S. Second Infantry
Division monument
on Omaha Beach
(Steinke family photo)

With Mike and Kelly Fortino on our balcony in Paris, June 2005
(Steinke family photo)

Ambassador Craig Stapleton (left), Marine Corps Ball, November, 2005 (Courtesy U.S. Embassy Paris)

Marine Corps Ball, November, 2005 (Steinke family photo)

Marine Corps Ball 2005, (L-R), Monica Potocnik, Col Edwin Potocnik, Austria; Lieut. Col Ben Moody, USA; Maureen Rousseau, Canada; Major General Vincent Desportes, France; Col Lorie Moody, USA; Susan and Col Georges Rousseau, Canada. (Steinke Family Photo)

In honor of
General Henri Roger Herve Jacques Bentegeat
Chief of Staff, French Armed Forces
and Mrs. Bentegeat

The Chairman of the Joint Chiefs of Staff
and Mrs. Richard B. Myers
request the pleasure of your company
at dinner
on Thursday, the eighth of September, two thousand and five
at seven o'clock
Quarters Six, Fort Myer, Virginia

R.S.V.P. by 31 August   *Business Suit*
(703) 695-4115
ocjcsprotocol@js.pentagon.mil

Invitation to the Chairman, Joint Chief of Staff Dinner in
honor of General Henri Bentegeat (Steinke family photo)

Major General Ken
Hunzeker presenting a
Certificate of Service to
Susan at our retirement
ceremony, U.S. Embassy,
Paris, June 2006
(Courtesy U.S. DAO Office)

Farewell luncheon, U.S. Ambassador's residence (L-R), Major General Brian Tarbet, USA; Lieutenant Colonel Thierry Delavaud, Major Olivier Lardans and Colonel (Ret) Charlie Deleris, France; Ambassador Craig Stapleton; Brigadier General Tim Gregson, UK; Captain (Navy) Wayne Haynes, Australia; Colonel Hans-Dieter Poth, Germany; Brigadier General Edwin Potocnik, Austria; and Colonel John Hynaas, Norway. (Courtesy U.S. Embassy Paris)

CHAPTER 21

NEW NATO COMMANDER VISITS PARIS

IT WAS A LATE MORNING in June 2003 as I arrived at Vélizy-Villacoublay airbase, about seven miles southwest of Paris. Known simply as *Villacoublay* by my fellow attachés in the DAO, the air base was not much to write home about. It did, however, have a large enough landing strip to accommodate aircraft like a C-130 and, taking a page from the construction of US Air Force bases, had a pretty darn good golf course for relatively low green fees. Established in 1911, the base was functional but otherwise unimpressive.

The airbase was also relatively secluded from the hustle and bustle of Paris. This made it a great place for visiting US and international VIPs who wanted to keep a low profile before entering Paris. Just a few weeks prior I had met a couple of high-ranking Pentagon officials here whom I had escorted to the secluded, away-from-the-press Bilderberg Conference at Versailles. The conference included a Davos-like list of elites from around the world. Their three-day agenda included European-American relations vis-à-vis Iraq and the Middle East, as well as terrorism, WMD-proliferation and other security challenges.

On this day in late June, however, I would meet the relatively new commander of the NATO Alliance's military forces, then totaling nineteen countries in all. General James "Jim" Logan Jones, Jr., the first and only Marine to be named NATO's *Supreme Allied Commander, Europe*, had already served as the US Marine Corps Commandant. By any measure, his résumé was exceptional. A graduate of Georgetown University's School of Foreign Service, he had led a Marine rifle platoon in combat in Vietnam, where he had been awarded the Silver Star and Bronze Star for Valor. He subsequently served as a US Senate liaison under a Navy captain named John McCain, and later led the Marine expeditionary unit that deployed to northern Iraq in 1991 to defend the Iraqi Kurds from the still viable and lethal Saddam Hussein. As I was soon to learn, General Jim Jones also spoke excellent French.

"Good morning, sir!" I said as I saluted the tall four-star general as he walked from his C-12 aircraft up to our waiting DAO armored car.

"Good morning, Colonel Steinke, how are things in Paris?" he queried.

"Well, as you know, sir, the political climate is not optimal, but we're doing well in spite of it," I replied.

"Well, it's good to be back in Paris," he stated as we got into the back seat of the Mercedes, he in the right rear seat and me taking the left.

As to his "back in Paris" comment, I thought perhaps he had been here before, but didn't give it much more thought. It would be about five months later, at the annual US embassy Marine corps ball in mid-November, where I would learn more details about Jones's experiences in Paris.

Giving us just enough time to get our seat belts fastened, our driver for this day, Georges Baron (Embassy support officer who was pinch-hitting for my regular driver, Thierry Fleuet), gave the thumbs-up to the ten or so gendarmes mounted on BMW 1200cc motorcycles near our car. The gendarmes then led us, sirens blaring, off the Villacoublay airbase. Our escort made easy work of our trip to Paris's *Ecole Militaire*, near the Eiffel tower and home to France's top man in uniform, General Henri Bentégeat.

"Rick," said Jones along the way, "I've been to a lot of places in Europe and beyond, but I believe these gendarmes are the best when it comes to motorcycle escort."

It was obviously not their first rodeo. They kept a consistent distance between each other and our vehicle, seeming to know exactly when to speed up, when to slow down, and when to change positions as we snaked through Paris's southwestern districts and streets. I had spent a little time in Italy and had also observed the Carabinieri, a paramilitary force similar to the gendarmes, in action more than once. I thought they were pretty darned good in their own right, so I had to ask.

"Even better than the Caribinieri, sir?" I queried.

"Yes, absolutely," he affirmed.

I would not learn until later just how much of an affinity Jones had for France and things French. As we cruised through the city, he let me in on something else.

"I want you to know that I intend to establish a strong professional, and even personal, relationship with General Henri Bentégeat," he stated, speaking of the French Chief of Defense. "As you know, we are going through some rough political waters right now, but the French armed forces are a major military partner, and while they are outside of NATO's integrated military command structure, they are *widely* deployed around the world, particularly in Africa and, of course, Afghanistan. We must be able to effectively work together."

"Roger that, sir," I responded. *Excellent*, I also thought, almost saying it out loud. Given the recent US-France political acrimony, a good relationship between Jones, America's top marine and NATO Commander, and Bentégeat, France's highest-ranking marine and person in uniform, would certainly not be bad for relations. French forces were not deployed in Iraq, but that was not by their own choice. They *were*, however, deployed in Afghanistan, and were *not* afraid to take casualties, unlike some other NATO allies, who hid behind every "caveat" to engaging in combat imaginable. (To be fair, in many cases they were constrained from combat, or at least offensive combat, by their respective parliaments.)

As we approached the *Ecole Militaire*, we bypassed the double wrought-iron gate that served as its public entrance and drove instead right up to the huge doors of the main *Ecole Militaire* building, part of which also served as Bentégeat's personal living quarters. Driving a few feet through the open doors and into the alcove, our driver stopped the Mercedes, and a French Army sergeant immediately opened Jones's door. Mine was then also opened, and I quickly came around the back of the car.

As he exited the car, a French colonel met Jones, and they departed the alcove with the colonel showing the way, entering the building through the adjacent wooden and glass doors. We then immediately proceeded up some broad stone steps, the same steps a young Napoleon Bonaparte had made his way while training here more than 200 years prior. Reaching the top of the steps, now just a few feet from the entrance to his quarters behind him, we met a waiting and broadly smiling General Bentégeat. He asked Jones warmly in French, "How are you, Jim?"

"I'm doing better now that I am back in Paris, Henri," responded Jones. From what I could tell, he did so with a near perfect French accent. "And you, Henri, how are you?"

"I am well," responded Bentégeat.

As we stepped into the French general's quarters, something of a spacious greeting room, accented by a beautiful crystal chandelier in the room's center, opened up to us. I could see out of the corner of my eye that this room led to a larger, well-appointed but not opulent living room to the left. I then pondered whom I would first engage, not looking forward to using my obviously not-so-perfect-as-Jim-Jones's French. In the meantime, I was quickly approached by a gentleman who stood out because he was not in uniform, like most of the other twenty or so people in the room were. Slightly shorter than me and in a business suit, he introduced himself.

"Hi, Colonel Steinke, I'm Charlie Deleris," said the smiling Frenchman in perfectly American-accented English, who I guessed was in his late fifties. "I've served with General Bentégeat for many years. I think he and General Jones are going to get along just fine. If you ever need anything, don't hesitate to ask," he added.

I was very thankful Deleris was speaking English in our first meeting, as I was a bit hesitant to speak what I knew was "lesser French" within earshot of General Jones. General Jones and I had barely known each other for an hour, and I didn't want him to have any early doubts about my ability to converse in French and do my job. I thought my French passable—certainly professionally so—but I did not yet have the confidence in it that I had in German and Italian. I found French—particularly the nasal French accent—to be much more difficult to mimic. To constantly improve, I would avail myself of a US embassy-provided tutor as often as I could during my first several months at the embassy.

As in previous similar circumstances to this point in my tour, I took note of the "don't hesitate to ask" point made by the close confidant of France's Chief of Defense. I'd heard the phrase by others before, but given the sincerity in Charlie's voice, I believed him. As it turned out, from their earliest days of military service, Colonel (Ret.) Charlie Deleris and General Henri Bentégeat knew and trusted each other through their long and distinguished military careers.

For my entire period of service in Paris, Deleris would be a great contact, engaging dinner guest, and friend. His English was so superior to my French that I rarely engaged him in French, about which he was very gracious and comfortable. On June 4, 2004, some eleven months after this first meeting, Deleris would be of immense help in rectifying a very awkward situation with a certain local mayor at the Omaha Beach cemetery, two days before the D-Day sixtieth anniversary ceremonies.

As the two general officers continued to speak, they stepped through the spacious living room, with its shiny, creaky wooden floorboards and high, chandeliered ceilings, toward the balcony facing the nearby and dominant Eiffel Tower. Seeing the big smiles on both Marine officers' faces, I was very confident the personal relationship that Jones was seeking with Bentégeat would be easily achieved.

CHAPTER 22

RELIGIOUS EXPERIENCES

IT IS NO SECRET THAT the life of a typical US military service member, between operational assignments and in-resident professional military education, requires constant moving. Averaged out over say a twenty-five-year career, it will include a dozen or more physical moves. That's about a dozen times soldiers may have to pull their kids out of school, leave familiar neighborhoods, and, if church-attending Christians as our family was, leave a local congregation as well. Some degree of trauma and sadness is usually involved, hopefully soon to be replaced by a new adventure and new friends.

Adjusting to a new environment can be challenging. It becomes even more so in a remote assignment, living in a foreign culture and having to communicate in a foreign language. That was the case for my wife, Susan, and me, within our first three years of marriage, as we lived for two years in a small village at the foothills of the Italian Piedmont mountains, in a place called *San Pietro val Lemina*. It was a couple of kilometers from the larger town of Pinerolo, and about a forty-minute drive from the larger, better-known city of Turin.

While living in a small village in the Piedmont foothills might sound adventurous, even idyllic to some, it isn't for everyone. My predecessor—and moreover, his wife and family (who spoke no

Italian)—had had such a challenging experience living there that they had departed the Army soon thereafter. However, Susan and I took it on as an adventure. She had fortunately been authorized to study Italian with me at the US Defense Language Institute in Monterey, California. But what would we do about church attendance? Since she had been raised Catholic and I Lutheran, and our Italian was not yet quite good enough for local churches, we settled on getting our weekly spiritual inspiration from Robert Schuller's weekly hour-long broadcast, the *Hour of Power*. It was fortunately carried by a local Italian television station every Sunday.

In Paris, we would not face that dilemma. There were numerous English-speaking churches, including St. Joseph's Roman Catholic Church, St. George's Anglican Church, St. John's Lutheran Church, the American Cathedral, and the American Church in Paris. Due to some friends' recommendations, we initially settled on the non-denominational American Church in Paris.

During one service at the church, which was often packed with people from everywhere (with a particularly large Philippine contingent), I was tapped on the shoulder by an usher. He motioned for me to follow him to the back of the church. As I got closer to the door, I spied a couple of French gendarmes, the senior of the two a major.

As I approached him, he had a troubled look on his face that did nothing to calm my already anxious disposition.

"Colonel Steinke," the major began in French, "may I see your French diplomatic ID card, just for verification purposes?"

"Sure thing," I said. With my heart rate now picking up, I pulled out the French government-provided ID card identifying me as accredited to the French Ministry of Defense.

"Do you own the silver Volkswagen Jetta wagon parked around the back of the church?" continued the major.

"Yes, I do," I responded.

"Well, it's illegally parked, and you have to move it immediately," he said.

"I will do that right now," I said.

As the major led me out the front doors of the church, which faced the Seine River on the *Quai d'Orsay*, we took a left turn and walked a few meters toward *Rue Jean Nicot*, then took another immediate left.

I then thought to myself, *Wow, I've been pulled out of church for a* parking *violation? It must be a slow day at headquarters.* At the moment, it made no sense.

Walking up Rue *Jean Nicot* with the river Seine at my back, as I reached the intersection with Avenue *Robert Schuman,* I made a final left turn toward my car.

I then took in a rather unsettling sight for what should have been a very calm Sunday morning: about six or seven gendarmes, some looking at me incredulously, others with a smirk, and still others with a very annoyed look. Behind my parked car, I could see their blue van. At this point the major explained what this scene was all about.

"Sir, you parked in front of the residence of the Ivory Coast Ambassador to France. Apparently, you did not see the two 'No Parking' signs flanking your car," stated the major.

"I must have missed them. I'm sorry about that," I replied.

I honestly did not remember if I had missed them, or if, running late to church (which seemed to be a family tradition), I had just ignored them, thinking whatever was written on them must not have applied on a Sunday morning.

"And, Colonel," the major said, pointing to the enclosed, gray, hard plastic ski carrier on top of the car, "that is what got our attention."

"Major, I am *very* sorry that my inattentiveness caused you to have call your people out here on a Sunday morning. Please convey that to your team. I feel like a complete jackass."

"It's no problem, sir," he said, fortunately with a slight smile, and headed to the parked van.

I slunk in the Volkswagen and moved it to a more suitable—this time completely legal—parking space about two blocks away.

As I walked back to the church, I pieced together what must have happened. My first mistake was obviously not reading and complying with the two "No Parking" signs, which, sure enough, my car fit perfectly between. Secondly, in 2003, the Ivory Coast Ambassador to France was not your average *Joe Ambassador to France*. Pretty much all hell had broken loose in the Ivory Coast, a former French colony with which France kept close ties, in the previous fall. Military rebels from the *Mouvement Patriotique de la Côte d'Ivoire* (MPCI, the Patriotic Movement of the Ivory Coast) had tried to overthrow the government, splitting the country in two. The MPCI occupied the northern half, and the southern half held the Ivorian government of President Laurent Gbagbo. Had the French government not quickly intervened with military force, the former West-African French colony, which had been an African model of stability and relative prosperity for the previous thirty years or so, might have been lost to the rebels.

Given the ongoing tension with the Ivory Coast, the French gendarmes, who had been notified by someone (perhaps a security guard inside the ambassador's residence?), must have suspected the ski box on top of my car could have contained a bomb. Hence, the French bomb squad was called out. Arriving at my car, they then must have tracked my license plate to the US Defense Attaché to France. Then somebody on the gendarmes bomb squad or back at the headquarters must have had enough smarts to realize that this American was probably attending the English-speaking church right around the block. I felt like an idiot, but fortunately, nothing further came of the incident.

I did, however, learn another lesson besides the one about reading parking signs. While, from a security perspective, I preferred that my family and I kept as low a profile as possible, I realized complete anonymity was not possible, even in a big city like Paris. Before the church usher had tapped me on the shoulder that morning, my family and I had only met perhaps a handful of the roughly 200 folks who might be attending a church service on any given Sunday. But somehow the gendarmes major was able to find out, fairly quickly, where I was seated in the church. I wasn't sure if that was comforting or troubling, although I was happy events had concluded the way they had. Had the gendarmes not found me, I'm not sure what condition that ski box, or my car, would have ended up in.

Several months later my family and I had a more benign but extraordinary experience in church, only this time it would be at the American Cathedral in Paris. It was on George V Avenue and closer to home for us, reducing our family timeliness challenge. And since I was raised a Lutheran, its Episcopalian and Anglican heritage was a bit more in my comfort range.

As I heard the Gospel Reading one morning in the Cathedral, it was as if an angel of heaven was speaking. Most Christians will understand me when I say that I felt as if the Holy Spirit was flowing through this—and I can't describe it any other way—*angelic* voice, which seemed to reverberate to every corner of the large cathedral. As I looked in the printed program for that Sunday's church service, I ran my finger down the page until I found the Scripture reading. The name beside it was Olivia de Havilland. I knew that Mrs. de Havilland was someone famous from the Hollywood of years gone by, but I did not instantly connect her name with that of "Melanie" from *Gone with the Wind*, one of the greatest movies of the twentieth century and the first film to win ten Academy Awards.

As Mrs. de Havilland continued to read, I pointed her name out to Susan. Susan's eyes widened, and she nodded, then leaned over and whispered, *"Gone with the Wind."* As I was to later learn, the British-American and two-time Oscar winner was a mainstay of the American Cathedral in Paris.

Since the late 1950s she has been an active, faithful, and highly respected church member in Paris.

I had never before, nor since, heard a voice like that in a worship service.

CHAPTER 23

DEADLY HEATWAVE

THE MOSTLY MILITARY BASTILLE DAY parade in Paris, held on July 14 every year, is practically a "must-show" event for the international military attachés accredited to France. Many of the senior attachés are seated in the large, official tribune at the end of the parade route, which runs along the *Champs-Élysées* and finishes at the *Place de la Concorde*. The Bastille Day parade serves as a sort of unofficial demarcation for when the summer vacation period in Paris begins to get serious. Once the Bastille Day passes, you can practically hear the *whoosh* as Parisians begin to head for the beaches, mountains, and distant lands for their almost sacrosanct summer vacations. In the last two weeks of August, along with most of the rest of Europe, the French summer vacation period reaches its crescendo.

My family and I decided to follow suit in July, after Bastille Day, taking our first summer vacation in France. We were fortunate to find a furnished apartment, owned by a US diplomat who had retired in Paris, on the island of Corsica and for a reasonable rate. The apartment was located in the northwest corner of the island, not far from the port town of Calvi.

As it turned out, the apartment—at the top of a large, three-story, rustic sandstone home—was a magnet for bats in the evening. At night, we had to open our windows to our non-air-conditioned bedrooms, mercifully allowing a bit of a sea breeze to come through after a day at the beach or touring the island, with temperatures reaching 95 degrees Fahrenheit. But open, screenless windows invited bats, which would swoop through one window, then fly across the room and out a window on the opposite side, diving perhaps three or four feet above our heads as we lay in bed. *I* would show the ladies how a real man responded to that trouble—by burying myself under the bedsheets as far as possible!

At the beach, our inflatable crocodile was the hit of the week, with Maria and Erika exchanging rides in the waves or arguing over who got to use it.

Corsica is the birthplace of Napoleon I, who was given the Italian name *Napoleone di Buonaparte* at birth. It was a magnificent island that took one back decades, if not centuries. This was due in part to the island's building codes, which prohibited the building of tall hotels along its beaches. I saw no structures, at least not modern ones, higher than four or five stories on this northeastern part of the island.

As the final quiet weeks of summer in Paris arrived in early August, so did the family of Susan's twin sister, Liza. Our travels included a weekend visit to some of the famous chateaus in the Loire Valley. Given France's deadly heat wave in the summer of 2003, the Loire could just as well have been called "Death Valley." After visiting the magnificent *Chenonceau* chateau on a particularly sweltering 102-degree day, we decided to check into our nearby hotel to escape the heat. Our motel had mentioned air-conditioning in its online advertisement, so we were very much looking forward to our respite.

As I walked into the motel's lobby, I realized it was stifling. There was no air-conditioning in the lobby, only a woefully inadequate fan. Was there air-conditioning perhaps in the rooms? I asked the middle-aged Frenchman behind the desk, and he quickly admitted that *"non,"* the motel did *not* have air-conditioned rooms. Although we had made a reservation, it was not yet 5:00 p.m., so I canceled it, turned on my heels, and departed.

"To heck with this," I told my brother-in-law Munzer. "If we are going to suffer, we might as well return to our apartment in Paris, rather than pay 150 euros per room to do it here." Our apartment in Paris was about two and a half hours away, so we decided to head home. At least our cars would be air-conditioned.

As we got to Paris in the early evening hours, the streets were quieter than normal, even for early August. You could practically see the heat rising up from the streets. When we got to our non-air-conditioned apartment, the outside temperature was over 100 degrees Fahrenheit. To get some air-flow going through the apartment, we strategically placed a couple of floor fans as best we could. That evening, at about 1:00 a.m., my brother-in-law and I, coincidentally within about five minutes of each other, found ourselves trying to sleep on the living room floor, next to a floor fan, seeking some relief. The unremitting temperatures, held in by the concrete of the city, made for a very long night and several long nights after that.

Extremely hot summers are not common to France, particularly in Paris and the northern areas. Consequently, the vast majority of homes and apartments had no air-conditioning, nor did most hospitals. In the fall, official government reports began to come out concerning this "heat wave of the century," which officially lasted from August 3 to August 13, 2003.

In France, there were 14,802 reported heat-related deaths (mostly among the elderly) during the heat wave, according to the French National Institute of Health. Morticians in Paris had run out of refrigeration space and had to resort to using commercial refrigeration facilities in and around Paris to store the dead. Doctors and family members were in their peak vacation periods, and sadly, many of the dead were not discovered until the return of their family members.

CHAPTER 24

REPAIRING RIFTS

AS FRANCE'S HEAT GAVE WAY to the cool nights and breezes of early September, activity began to pick up at the embassy. It was virtually impossible to get anything done with French counterparts in August, so I was happy to see we were returning to a more productive period. My first year as army attaché and then defense and army attaché had been a topsy-turvy affair, one that I would never have predicted before assuming my duties.

From a diplomatic standpoint, particularly a US-France, military-to-military diplomatic standpoint, the previous six months had been all about "punishing France" for their "failure" to join the American-led war effort in Iraq. Being at the leading edge of that policy was not what I would call fun—nor was it professionally satisfying. Besides what has already been described in the preceding months, the French were denied, after many years of joint participation, from participating in the US Air Force's 2004 Red Flag exercise, the top live-flight training exercise in the Air Force. Later, French journalists who dared to show up without visas at a gaming expo in Las Vegas were reported to have been *handcuffed* and returned to their country, with other adversarial activities at various levels reported as well. Although I never verified this, there was a rumored denial of a visit to the United States by General Bentégeat. (The rumored visit was not coordinated through my office, but instead would have been coordinated through the French defense attaché's office in Washington, D.C.) Nonetheless, with Leach's steady, on-the-scene leadership in Paris, things didn't get out of hand, at least not on the European side of the Atlantic.

In late August and about a week prior to the embassy and our French counterparts being at or near full staffing, Leach wanted to talk "strategy." After getting a call from his executive assistant, Ms. Lowe, I reported to Ambassador Leach's office.

"Good morning, Mr. Ambassador, good to see you," I said.

"Good morning, Rick, good to see you as well," he replied. "I hope you got some time off with your family this summer."

"I did, sir, and thank you for asking. Corsica turned out to be pretty cool, at least in the evenings, and was otherwise a very interesting place to visit," I said.

"I understand, Rick," he said. "It was a pretty hot one this year. If anything, if it wasn't *too* hot, it ought to be a good year for wine," he said. (At this point, the rumors concerning French deaths from the heat wave had not yet begun to swirl, and official accounts would still take weeks to reach the French people and the public, so the ambassador's remark about wine was not off-color or callous in any way.)

"Absolutely, sir, perhaps even on par with the year 2000," I replied, referring to a great vintage year for Bordeaux wines in particular.

"Maybe," he said, and added with a wink, "but they'll never be as good as California wines." (Ambassador Howard Leach was a man who always promoted "America," and the only wines he served in the ambassador's residence—and that I served at home, lest the reader think I'd gone native—were always California or US wines.)

I nodded.

"Rick, I think this 'punish France' business has gone on about long enough, and I think it's time to begin bridging the divide," he said.

"What do you have in mind, sir?" I asked.

"Well, I'm considering hosting a dinner for Minister Alliot-Marie and some of the top brass of the French Armed Forces. What are your thoughts on that?"

"Mr. Ambassador, I think that's a brilliant idea."

I was relieved that this adversarial relationship with the French, of which the French Ministry of Defense and Armed Forces had received the brunt, might soon be changing for the better.

"Whom do you think I should invite?" he asked.

"Sir, besides Madame Alliot-Marie, the invitation list should definitely include the CHOD, General Bentégeat, and the service chiefs. There are also a handful of other key folks, such as Lieutenant General Michel Masson, the head of the French Defense Intelligence Agency, and perhaps Genereal Bentégeat's deputy, Vice-Admiral Alain Coldefy, who frequently addresses and interacts with the attachés, who should be considered."

"Well, Rick, I value your advice. Our protocol folks are going to be in touch to make sure we've got some of our key MOD and military interlocutors joining us for the dinner," he said.

"Sir, I appreciate it and look forward to it," I responded.

A few weeks later, I would enter the spectacular US Ambassador's Residence at 41 rue *du Faubourg Saint-Honoré*. Built between 1852 and 1855, the magnificent limestone-façade, three-story mansion came into the hands of the great bankers of the day in 1876, the Rothschild family. Edmond Rothschild had had it remodeled and expanded to its current floor layout. The garden, perfect for large parties and diplomatic gatherings, was about the size of an American football field. In early 1940, however, the Rothschilds fled Paris in advance of the Nazi invasion, and Hermann Göring turned the mansion into an officers' club for the Luftwaffe. After World War II the Allies rented it for three years, until the American government purchased it in 1948.

Entering through the Residence's impressive marbled entry hall, I was directed by a protocol officer to the Louis XVI Salon, with its period furnishings and Empire chandelier. This was one of three salons—or in perhaps more relatable (at least for me) bourgeois language—"living rooms" of the mansion. I was surprised to see about thirty people already gathered there, standing and conversing while drinking mostly champagne and wine. About another twenty or so would soon follow behind me into the residence. This was obviously not going to be a small dinner. To lower the formality, the attire for the evening was business suits for the men, with the ladies in cocktail dresses, rather than military uniform, tuxedo, or evening gowns.

As I moved into the crowd, I put a greeting hand out to some familiar faces, including the chief of staff of the French Army, General Bernard Thorette. Of everyone there, I was particularly glad to see him, since roughly five months prior I had spoken to him to deliver the initial brunt of the "punish France" policy, when our US Marine War College canceled coming to his reception, a reception that had been weeks in the planning. I also said hello to some of the lower-ranking but more familiar French Ministry of Defense and General Staff officials with whom I had more frequent contact.

After about forty minutes or so of drinks and small talk, we were signaled to move up the broad marble staircase to the family dining room, where there were five to six tables of ten people each, with a separate and slightly larger one reserved for the ambassador and his special guests, including French Minister of Defense Michèle Alliot-Marie. Covering most of one wall of the family dining room was an exquisite eighteenth-century Flemish tapestry depicting the life of Moses and entitled *The Worship of the Golden Calf*, attributed to Gaspard Van Der Borght.

At the appropriate point in the dinner, Leach made welcoming remarks, beginning with an acknowledgment of Minister Alliot-Marie's presence. His remarks focused on the long-standing ties, particularly military ties, that our two republics had had for well over 200 years. Besides mentioning the French heroes of the American Revolution, such as the Marquis de Lafayette and Comte de Rochambeau, Leach also mentioned the Lafayette Escadrille, composed of American pilots who ventured to France during World War I to serve under French command, thus repaying in their own way the American debt to France from the American Revolution.

As I looked around the room, I saw mostly smiling faces, with a few, of course, still skeptical of American intentions. After months of their getting denied and disparaged by the American "punish the French" policy, I certainly did not expect euphoria and smiling faces everywhere. It would take some time to rebuild cordiality and trust at the highest levels. Nonetheless, I thought Leach's words hit the mark for a brighter future and improved cooperation, ending, as he always did with "*Vive la France, Vivent les Etats Unis!*"

Within a few weeks, in late November, one US "punish France" act by the DoD struck closer to home. This act exemplified the depth of the administration's annoyance—and perhaps even outright anger—with the French. Each year (or at least in most years) the US Congress determines the budget and expenditures for the entire US Department of Defense and Armed Forces. To do so, it passes into law the National Defense Authorization Act. For the National Defense Authorization Act of Fiscal Year 2004, under H.R. 1588 (108th Congress), Title V, MILITARY PERSONNEL POLICY, Section 503, there was some very specific language about the position of US Defense Attaché to France:

"REPEAL OF REQUIRED GRADE OF DEFENSE ATTACHE IN FRANCE. (a) IN GENERAL- Section 714 of title 10, United States Code, is repealed."

Section 714, of title 10, US Code, specified that a flag or general officer was to serve in the position of US defense attaché to France. This new law essentially repealed that requirement, henceforth assigning a colonel to the position.

As the months continued, the French were mostly, but not completely, out of the doghouse. One indicator was the degree to which senior US officers came to France. Outside of Great Britain, on the European continent, the French ranked relatively high in terms of US military relations and respect. Given that France was a major political as well as military ally, it was not unusual for very senior-ranking US officers to make a stop in France at least once during their typically three-year tours, or in the case of the service chiefs, four-year tours. During my first three years in Paris only one service chief and the chairman of the joint chiefs of staff, General Richard Myers traveled over. Air Force chief of staff General John Jumper visited relatively early on. Marine Corps commandant General Michael Hagee, enroute to the hallowed Marine ground at Belleau Wood, also came to Paris during the latter part of my tour.

Not a service chief, General Bryan D. Brown, commander of US Special Operations Command (USSOCOM or often abbreviated to "SOCOM"), however, visited twice. The reason he did so was the close working relationship between US and French special forces in Afghanistan, as well as in several places on the African continent. General Bentégeat would later return the favor with a trip to USSOCOM headquarters in Tampa, Florida. General Brown also got to know the French special forces commander, Brigadier General Bernard Puga, quite well.

Before the month of September 2003 was over, however, there would be another sign of an olive branch being extended to the French government by the Bush Administration: a visit to Paris by First Lady Laura Bush.

CHAPTER 25

FIRST LADY
LIGHTS UP PARIS

"RICK, THIS IS BRANDY," SAID the ambassador's executive assistant on the phone.

"Hi, Brandy, what can I do for you today?" I asked.

"Howard is traveling out to Le Bourget Airport tomorrow night to meet a VIP," she said. "And he'd like you to accompany him. Are you free then?"

After a quick look at my calendar, I declared, "I am indeed."

"Good," she replied. "Stop by the office and I'll give you the details."

I thought perhaps the VIP might be the chairman of the joint chiefs of staff, or maybe the secretary of defense, who was making an impromptu stop in Paris, perhaps on their way to Afghanistan or Iraq. But then again, I expected I would have been fully appraised in advance of either person visiting.

When I got to Brandy's desk, she provided the details.

"The ambassador is going out to meet First Lady Laura Bush tomorrow night. He'd like you to go with him. He will leave directly from the Residence at 9:30 p.m. Just meet him there a bit earlier, as usual," she said.

"Is anybody else going?" I asked.

"With Howard? No, you are the only one. There will be some embassy support people out there to bring her back in a separate vehicle, but it will just be you and Howard riding together."

"Wow, okay . . . thanks," I responded.

I wasn't quite sure why I got the nod to go with Leach to meet the First Lady, but I was certainly intrigued and, quite frankly, thrilled.

Arriving ten minutes before the ambassador's scheduled departure from the mansion on *rue du Faubourg Saint-Honoré*, as I normally did when riding with him to a venue, I chatted outside with the driver and security detail members. It was a mild fall evening in Paris.

At 9:29, the ambassador walked out and greeted us all. We briskly moved to his blue 700-series BMW. While the embassy had an armored Cadillac as well, the top-of-the-line and armored BMW was one of several purchased by the US State Department at a discount and assigned to several embassies in Europe. I had already had the privilege of riding in the BMW with Leach a couple of times before, but this night, it was, well, about to become a special ride.

As we followed our lead security vehicle with blaring blue siren on top, a trail vehicle behind us, we made it through the streets of Paris in very short order. There were two things that were about to make this evening very special, and for an Army sergeant's kid from a small town in Michigan, downright cool: speed . . . and meeting the First Lady.

Within minutes, we were on Paris's *périphérique*, the bypass that encircles the entire city, headed for Le Bourget Airport. Le Bourget is a secondary international airport to the main international airport, Charles de Gaulle. It has an Air and Space Museum on the premises, and every second year it is the site of the Paris Air Show. Occasionally, VIP aircraft would also use this airport to land in Paris. Some seventy-six years prior, perhaps its biggest VIP landing would be accomplished by Charles Lindbergh, after his record-setting trans-Atlantic flight. On the night of Sunday, September 28, 2003, it would be First Lady Laura Bush arriving.

Before I knew it, on a fairly dark night and stretch of highway after we had left the périphérique's tall lamp posts, we were going very, very fast. I can't be sure how fast because, as much as I wanted to, I couldn't quite see the speedometer from the back seat. But my guess, having been on the French *autoroute* and German *autobahn* many times at fairly high speeds, was that we were doing at least ninety miles per hour, perhaps more. I looked over at the ambassador and he was nonplussed. I figured either we were doing this for security reasons, or we were late. In any case, it was the fastest I'd ever traveled—legally or otherwise—on a French road.

The purpose of Laura Bush's visit, according to the ambassador, was for the United States to rejoin UNESCO, the United Nations Educational, Scientific, and Cultural Organization. (I did not know that the United States had withdrawn from UNESCO, but I was not about to let Leach know that.) The average American citizen, at least those who have traveled a bit, probably knows UNESCO as the organization that moves around the world preserving some of the world's greatest physical treasures and places, among other things. There had been a nineteen-year absence from UNESCO by the US, dating back to when the Reagan Administration had determined it to be "corrupt and anti-American."

As the ambassador and I pulled up on the side of the runway, the First Lady's plane was just landing. After a short taxi, the mobile staircase was emplaced, and within minutes the door at the top of the steps opened and a spotlight came on. Somebody who must have been a member of the Secret Service exited the door and descended the steps first. The First Lady was not far behind.

As Laura Bush descended the steps and reached Leach, he greeted her with a warm, "Good evening, and welcome to Paris!"

"Well, Howard, it is just wonderful to be here," she said.

Turning to me, Leach said, "Laura, I'd like you to meet our defense attaché, Colonel Rick Steinke."

"Colonel, it's very nice to meet you," she said.

"Ma'am, it's my honor and pleasure to meet you," I replied. "And welcome to Paris."

"Thank you!"

With that, the ambassador and I led the First Lady, as we walked perhaps 150 feet or so while engaging in small talk, to her designated vehicle for our trip back to the ambassador's residence.

As I rode back to the residence with the ambassador, I could only think of one thing: that Laura Bush had an aura, perhaps even a spirit, of genuine kindness and decency about her. I had rarely come across that in this world. I sensed that after only a few minutes in her presence. Perhaps some readers might take that as a bit of fawning, but quoting Olivia de Havilland, who later in life described her response to her *Gone with the Wind* role as Melanie, "It was her character that attracted me the most—because of her admirable qualities and values that meant so much to her." That's what I felt, and I'm pretty sure those who she came in contact with in Paris the next day, including President Jacques Chirac, felt the same thing.

First Lady Laura Bush's visit and diplomatic mission to UNESCO and Paris were hailed by the great majority of French news outlets to have been a great success. Was her visit perhaps another US olive-branch gesture beyond Leach's recently completed dinner with the French minister of defense and top military leadership? Perhaps . . . but only more time would tell.

CHAPTER 26

TURKEY, THE MARINE CORPS BALL . . . AND A FIRE

FOR OUR FAMILY, NOVEMBER WAS more than just a time to commemorate Veteran's Day and celebrate Thanksgiving—Maria's birthday was also on Veteran's Day. However, for US military attachés and diplomats assigned to a US embassy somewhere in the world, especially the larger embassies, there is another traditional celebration observed on or about November 10: the US Marine Corps Birthday Ball. In an embassy as large as US Embassy Paris, with a contingent of roughly a dozen Marines assigned at any given time, it was a grand affair. For US military attachés and diplomats, it was also a good opportunity for hosting local-host-nation or international friends and guests, while exposing them to a great American tradition.

For this evening, I hosted French Vice Admiral Alain Coldefy, French joint staff director of international relations; Mr. Colin Cameron, a Scot who was the former secretary general of the by then-defunct West European Union; Mr. Rick Spann, an American businessman with the Colgate Company; and Lieutenant Colonel Thierry Delavaud, a French gendarme officer and aide-de-camp to French minister of defense Michèle Alliot-Marie; and their lovely ladies.

The 228th US Embassy Paris Marine Corps Birthday Ball, held on November 15th, 2003, in the upscale Intercontinental Hotel Le Grand (built in 1862), was exceptional, as the evening's guest speaker turned out to be the top US Marine in uniform, General Jim Jones, supreme allied commander, Europe. Shortly after arriving at the Intercontinental, although not a Marine, I thought it my duty as the senior military officer of US Embassy Paris to welcome and say hello to Jones.

"Sir, thank you so much for coming to Paris for this special event," I said.

"Rick, I've, of course, been to a lot of these over the years," he said. "But this one is pretty special indeed. I know a little something about Paris, and even this hotel. When I was a toddler, my father was a businessman, and he moved our family to Paris. We actually stayed in this hotel before moving to our local home. I went on to grow up in Paris."

"Sir, I had no clue," I said.

"And I'll tell you something else," he said. "After 'The Star-Spangled Banner,' the Marseillaise gets my heart beating pretty darn well."

The Marseillaise was the French national anthem. *Voila!* I thought. *No wonder his French is so good!*

Understanding more about Jones and why he had felt so at ease and gained such respect among the French, I returned to my wife, Susan, and our colorful guests for the evening. The ceremonies that followed were very dignified, honoring the Marines serving at the US Embassy, as well as the Marines serving around the world, particularly those in harm's way in Afghanistan and Iraq. The oldest and youngest Marines present were also recognized. General Jones gave a great speech, during which he revealed to the 200 or so guests what he told me earlier that evening: that he had grown up in Paris.

I later learned Jim Jones had been a standout basketball player for the local international high school, the American School of Paris. His leadership and athletic skill took that team farther in competition than it had ever gone before. I further learned he had gone on to play basketball for Georgetown University in Washington, D.C.

After the ceremonies were complete, and I had started in on my main course, Mr. Jess Presas, a retired Marine Corps sergeant major and the US Transportation Security Agency (TSA) liaison officer to France and Morocco, came over to our table. Jess, whose family shared our apartment building stairwell, calmly whispered in my ear, "Rick, apparently there was a fire in your place, but everything is okay. The Chilean defense attaché has been trying to call you."

I immediately reached in my pocket for my cell phone, and sure enough, there had been two phone calls from the new Chilean defense attaché, Colonel Carlos Stuardo Escobar, whose family had moved into the apartment right below ours. I immediately called him.

"Hallo," he answered.

"Carlos, hello, this is Rick . . . I understand there has been a *fire?*" I asked, my heart beating a bit faster than normal.

"Yes, Rick, but everybody is okay. Not to worry, everyone is *okay*. The kids are at the Presas residence. Your apartment is closed, but you can go in when you come home, and you can sleep there. There was a small fire in the kitchen," he said.

"A fire in the kitchen? But everyone is *fine?*" I asked.

"Yes, *everyone,* including the dog," he said. "Don't worry. Take your time and have fun at the ball."

"Carlos, many, many thanks for the information. Adios," I said.

"Have a good evening," he responded.

As I put the cell phone back in my pocket, I leaned over and whispered to Susan, "We had a small fire in the apartment, but everyone is perfectly okay. We don't have to bolt out now, but once we finish our dessert, I think we should be on our way."

Not wanting to startle our guests, I looked up but said nothing at that moment, trying to be as poker-faced as possible. However, as we finished our meal, I had to let everyone know that we needed to go home. Mr. Cameron later remarked that my calm right after the phone call was a "remarkable display of *sangfroid*." I did not know whether to take that as a compliment, since kids were involved. But since I'd had several assurances from the Chilean defense attaché that the family and babysitter were fine, I resolved not to worry about it further. But as we drove home, of course I worried what we would learn once there, as did Susan.

As we returned to our apartment, there was—somewhat surprisingly—almost no lingering smell of smoke. Our kitchen, however, was covered in a fine blue powder. Thanks to an American couple who lived above us and had insisted on pitching in, we were able to clean all the powder within about an hour. The oven glass on the front of our stove had been broken, and the stove was disconnected from its gas source on the wall. The fire turned out to be a family saga about which *all* the facts did not come out for a few years, but we were finally able to piece together the full account of what happened.

That evening, Erika, Maria, and our golden retriever, Lucky, were in the apartment with a fiftysomething lady we had habitually used as a babysitter and for occasional help with housecleaning. At one point in the evening the girls noticed Lucky pacing rapidly—almost frantically—back and forth, occasionally barking. But they had no way of knowing what was bothering him. Our babysitter did not react and might even have been snoozing. Finally, thank God, Erika looked up in the TV room—which was separated from the kitchen by about ten feet of hallway—and noticed smoke billowing near the door. Having just passed her twelfth birthday the previous month, she immediately ran downstairs and pounded on the apartment door of our concierge, Mr. Cousin. Mr. Cousin promptly called the Paris Fire Brigade, and then ran back up the stairs with Erika. He immediately disconnected the stove from its gas source and pulled it from the wall, then got our babysitter, Maria, Erika, and Lucky out of the apartment

The Paris Fire Department is not your average fire department, French or otherwise. Dating back to the days of Napoleon I, Paris firefighters uniquely belong to the French Army, and are organized as the *Paris Fire Brigade*, with an excellent reputation established over roughly 200 years of responsiveness, competency, and bravery. The *Marseille Naval Fire Battalion* is the only other firefighting unit in France that belongs to a military service, the Navy.

The Paris Fire Brigade responded within minutes, having their fire-arresting equipment up the stairs and in our kitchen in a jiffy. As we were to learn years later, in their support van, the firefighters also tested Erika and our babysitter for smoke inhalation. They determined by the strength of six-year-old Maria's crying that her lungs were just fine.

The fire had inadvertently been started by our babysitter. She felt culpable over the entire affair, but we later tried to assure her that it was not her fault. Just the day prior to the fire, Susan and I had hosted an annual Thanksgiving luncheon for about thirty international women, mainly the spouses of French military officers and international military attachés assigned to Paris. I had baked a big turkey—probably a little over twenty pounds—for the event, and the spouses of our US military attachés had also pitched in with side dishes and cleanup.

Right before this traditional luncheon, I always explained the American Thanksgiving story, concluding it with a Thanksgiving prayer on behalf of the group. After the event, the US spouses helped clean up. But one item to be cleaned got overlooked: the oven. At the very bottom of it lay, not easily discernible to the naked eye, what must have been a small layer of grease. I later recalled that the tin container that held the turkey had been full to the brim with grease, so some could have very easily spilled over and into the bottom of the oven.

As it turned out, the evening of the fire, our babysitter had noticed the oven needed cleaning. Wanting to be helpful, she decided to turn the oven's automatic, heat-inducing cleaner on and then go watch TV with the girls. It takes little imagination to figure out what happened not long after that.

A couple of days later, I was walking Lucky in our neighborhood when I came across a stove, almost identical to ours, with its glass window shattered and black marks on the white surface around the broken glass window. The stove was on the curb of the street, ready for trash pickup. With just a twinge of schadenfreude, I felt better knowing we were not the only ones who had almost burned up our kitchen, or worse. Seven years later, we returned to visit our old neighborhood, and we learned from Mr. Cousin that our apartment had been abandoned—because of a fire.

CHAPTER 27

CONGRESSIONAL DELEGATIONS

IF ONE SERVES IN A US embassy abroad long enough, particularly one associated with a major ally such as US Embassy Paris, one can expect to experience visits by members of the US Congress. Generally speaking, I believe the great majority of these visits, as long as they involve valid, on-the-ground and information-seeking objectives, are well worth the expenditure of American tax dollars. Several years ago, US members of Congress were ridiculed for the fact that about one-third of the members did not own a US passport and had never traveled outside the United States.

As Mark Twain once wrote, "Travel is fatal to prejudice, bigotry, and narrow-mindedness, and many of our people need it sorely on these accounts. Broad, wholesome, charitable views of men and things cannot be acquired by vegetating in one little corner of the earth all one's lifetime."

While serving at US Embassy Paris I was involved in hosting and also briefing several US Congressional Delegations (referred to as CODELs), ranging from one member of the US House of Representatives to as many as seven US senators, at about the time the US was initiating coalition operations against Iraq. Some of the visits were memorable.

Sometimes CODELs, or particularly individual members of Congress, have an ax to grind. They are only looking for information to support their preconceived—and often politicized—notions. On other occasions, the member or members come in completely open-minded, ready to let the informational and analytical chips fall where they may, or the evidence lead to wherever it may lead. A visit by Senators Orrin Hatch (R-UT) and Saxby Chambliss (R-AL) was of the latter variety.

As the senior US defense representative to France, it was my job to brief members of Congress on the state of France's military forces, as well as our US-France military relations, our common joint military operations around the world and intelligence sharing, for example. Occasionally, especially when asked, I would stray over into France's political-military policies and approaches vis-à-vis Europe and the United States, although congressional members could just as well have heard about that from an embassy political officer.

I was not a resident of the state of Utah, but I was a frequent visitor and had long thought Hatch one of our more thoughtful and articulate senators. In his visit with Chambliss, he did not disappoint, asking questions with a sincere interest in hearing the evidence, versus someone who thought they knew it all. Chambliss, who was quite a bit junior to Hatch in terms of experience and "tenure" at the time, approached my two-on-one "deskside" briefing in a similar fashion. A couple of other CODEL visits, however, did not go as well. For these, I will not name names.

One of the old adages one hears from certain members of Congress is that many allies within the NATO Alliance do not pick up their fair share of defense expenditures or force readiness. This adage is not without merit. An objective review of allied defense spending will demonstrate exactly that for most nations in the Alliance. Over the years, the degree to which Congress—as well as presidents and secretaries of defense—have criticized the underperformance of allied nations in the military readiness realm has ebbed and flowed. When Congress's frustration has been at its peak, the cry often heard was: "If our European allies don't carry more of their share for NATO's defense, we will withdraw US forces from Europe!"

On one occasion, two senior senators came to Paris wanting to meet with the French chief of defense. This request was a bit unusual, as the great majority of the members of Congress who were seeking direct contact with a foreign defense official would request to see the civilian, politically appointed head of the Armed Forces, normally the minister of defense (which seven senators had previously done just prior to war with Iraq). They rarely ask to meet with the top person in military uniform.

In this case, the two senators had more than fifty years of senate service between them, so I was quite confident they would be on sure footing as they personally met with France's chief of defense (US chairman, JCS-equivalent), General Henri Bentégeat.

During the meeting, essentially an informal, deskside briefing by General Bentégeat, the general, senators, and I were the only ones in Bentégeat's office. The two senators (we'll call them Senators Adams and Smith) came in hell-bent to extract an additional commitment from Bentégeat, mostly in the way of a military commitment to Iraq. However, things did not go quite the way they had envisioned. The conversation, held in English, closely approximated this:

"Thank you for taking the time to host us, General," said Senator Adams.

"It is my pleasure to do so, Senator. How can I help you gentlemen? Is there anything specific concerning the French Armed Forces you'd like me to tell you about?" asked General Bentégeat.

"Well, there is, General. What we'd really like to hear about is how you can contribute more to NATO's defense and to coalition operations, particularly in Afghanistan and in Iraq. We believe France could do more. The US Congress is considering pulling US troops out of Europe if more is not done by our Allies," said Senator Smith.

Taking the senators' broadside with a calm demeanor, General Bentégeat began to tick off all the places where France was contributing to NATO's missions, such as the Balkans, as well as some other places in the world, such as Africa, which were essentially devoid of a Western military presence, except where French and American forces were deployed in restoring or keeping the peace. General Bentégeat then continued:

"Well, gentlemen, let me just say that after the horrible 9/11 attacks on the United States, France was among the first countries to enter the fight against al Qaeda. In the autumn of 2001 we sent several combat aircraft, as well as the French 21st Marine Regiment on land and several ships at sea. We also deployed over 200 Special Forces from our Special Forces Brigade to conduct operations against the Taliban. Even though the United States did not invoke NATO's Article 5, France responded quickly, and I believe effectively, and I expect we will continue to do so in Afghanistan."

"Well, General . . . okay, go ahead," said Senator Adams.

"And on the African continent, we are heavily engaged in places like Djibouti, where we operate closely with your Marines in the *Combined Joint Task Force-Horn of Africa*. We also have a military presence in the Ivory Coast, Chad, Senegal, and other places," said General Bentégeat. "Our current deployments include over 14,000 military forces worldwide. As to Iraq, that was, of course, a political decision, which I think you understand."

"Well, we do understand it was *not* a military decision, is that correct?" asked Senator Smith, either seeking redundant confirmation or missing what General Bentégeat had just said.

"No, Senator, it was a political one," answered General Bentégeat.

While the two senators were certainly right to question the great degree to which the United States was carrying NATO's defense load (spending 3.4% of GDP in 2003 for defense and carrying over 70% of NATO's overall load) for Europe and North America, France was the wrong target of their frustration. What General Bentégeat did *not* say was that France was contributing 2.6% of its GDP to defense, ahead of the United Kingdom (2.4%), Germany (1.4%) and Canada (1.2%), and was behind only the United States, Turkey (3.7%), and Greece (4.2%), with the latter two countries spending those relatively high percentages more as deterrents to *each other* rather than in support of the Alliance as a whole. In other words, if you took out Greece and Turkey, France in 2003 was second to the United States in NATO nation defense spending as a percentage of gross domestic product.

The meeting concluded cordially, with General Bentégeat thanking them for their interest in the French Armed Forces and the two senators thanking him for taking time to brief them.

In another CODEL, a certain member of Congress came in with an ax to grind, *looking* for places to disparage the French, and not only the French, but the effectiveness of some of our attachés in performing their duties. In response to this Congressman's approach, I can only say I followed an adage by a former senator and friend whom I met at Harvard's Kennedy School in 1998, Al Simpson of Wyoming: "When in doubt, fight 'em with the facts!"

Two other members of Congress, one a Democrat, the other a Republican and traveling *together*, turned out to not only be relatively well-informed but clearly disposed to learn more. They also seemed to like each other. (Imagine that today!) Further, they took a personal interest in my family. When I asked if they might write personal notes to my daughter Erika, who had just started a new school year, they happily obliged.

"Erika, Study hard in school and listen to your dad," wrote Bill Shuyster, representative from Pennsylvania's 9th congressional district.

"Erika, Good luck at school!," penned Tim Ryan from Ohio's 13th congressional district.

As I held—and still hold—the majority of our citizen-representatives in high regard, I was gratified they took time for such simple but personal gestures.

Another visit included a breakfast in the ambassador's residence with Senator Joe Biden (D-DE). At the time of his visit, Biden had just completed a six-year run as the ranking minority member of the Senate Foreign Relations Committee. At the breakfast, I was a couple of seats away from him, so I was not able to engage in continuous conversation. But as the breakfast concluded, we stood up and walked over to me, patting me on the shoulder.

"Hey, Colonel, I understand that when we went to war in Iraq, we were only about thirty days away from the French having joined us in the coalition. Was that your take too?" he asked.

"Yes, sir, it was," I responded. "There was no way to guarantee that, but I do know that the French Armed Forces were preparing three courses of action in the way of contributions to the coalition: 7,000, 9,000, and 15,000 troops, or thereabouts. Once President Chirac told them to shut it down, I never heard another thing about Iraq War preparations."

"Well, I did not know that about the numbers," said Senator Biden. "But they sure do make sense in terms of what I understood about the French almost joining the coalition. They apparently just needed more time."

CHAPTER 28

VALLEE BLANCHE

THE FRENCH *ÉCOLE MILITAIRE DE Haute Montagne* (High Mountain Military School) is a French Army specialized military training organization located in the French alpine town of Chamonix. The school trains French and allied military personnel in arctic and mountain warfare, mountain leadership and survival, rock climbing, and skiing. Each year I served as defense attaché, the French Army Staff sent out invitations to select defense, Army, or Marine attachés assigned to Paris to attend a one-week mountain warfare orientation and training course at the school.

In effect, the event ended up being more orientation than actual training, including one day of mountain survival, movement techniques, and mountain warfare orientation. That was followed by three days of skiing in the French Alps. The four-day affair was a great bonding experience not only with our French military colleagues but other international military attachés assigned to Paris as well.

In 2004, there was an added feature to the week's schedule: for volunteers, there was an invitation to ski one of the more challenging stretches of off-piste and crevassed-marked stretches of glacier on the planet: the Vallee Blanche (White Valley). The backcountry glacier was completely ungroomed and constantly changing, with new crevasses from a few to hundreds of feet deep appearing and disappearing almost monthly, if not weekly. Personal mountain guides were strongly recommended. As advertised, the appropriate level of skiing ability was from "strong intermediate to expert."

I later learned that some Valle Blanche websites provide a personal capabilities assessment checklist, which mentioned things like one's ability to ski moguls. (Imagine a steep mountain slope full of round and uneven speed bumps. That's what a mogul field is like.) I missed the part about being able to ski moguls before I signed up to ski the Valle Blanche.

"So, Rick, are you going to join us for our trip through the Valle Blanche?" asked my good friend and Austrian Army colonel, Edwin Potocnik.

"Edwin, do you think my skiing level is up to it?" I asked.

"Of *course* it is!" he promptly answered.

"Well, I consider myself a high intermediate skier, but not an expert," I said to Potocnik, who clearly *was* an expert.

Of the twenty-five or so international attachés gathered for the week, only about five were expert-level (one was the president of our International Attaché Association, the Swiss lieutenant general and former Swiss Army chief of staff Jacques Dousse).

Of the five, Potocnik was far and away the best. "Look, Rick, we will have a guide out there, and we will stay together. No big deal."

"Uh, okay . . . count me in." I tried to sound as enthusiastic, decisive, and confident as possible, but felt none of those three things.

The www.chamonixskiguide.com website underlines this text, and only this text, out of every page on its website:

"Attention to not come with a friend to please her or him and end in a trap, it's frequent."

This was a direct English translation from French, so I will paraphrase:

Do not [ski the Vallee Blanche] just because you want to please a friend. Doing so often ends in a "trap"... at the bottom of a crevasse.

By saying "yes" to Potocnik, who made skiing look easier than a walk in the park, I had just ignored that warning.

Serving in the US Army, particularly in the latter half of my twenty-eight years of active service, I often saw "risk assessments" used to enforce safety and minimize risk to soldiers. (In the later years, some commanders bemoaned this policy as too bureaucratic and overly cautious, particularly in non-combat tours or areas.) Had I been objective, I would have given myself a failing grade in my personal risk assessment. I thought I was a pretty decent but not great skier, and I didn't have a clue about what I'd be getting into in the Valle Blanche.

As the morning of the Valle Blanche adventure arrived, five of us gathered, along with our local French guide (we'll call him Gilles): Major Ales Klepek, Czech Republic; Lieutenant Colonel Raimond Nitiss, Estonia; Commander Magnus Westerlund, Sweden; my buddy, Colonel Edwin Potocnik of Austria; and me. Arriving in our van at the base of the Aigulle du Midi cable car with Gilles at the wheel, we found out Gilles was a third-generation mountain guide. This quieted my slightly anxious heart a bit. After we parked, we offloaded our skis and rucksacks of varying sizes. Gilles pulled out a cardboard box from the back of the van. It was full of harnesses.

"Gentlemen, please put these on. If you have any questions about how to adjust them, just ask," said Gilles.

Looking at the harnesses, I could see they were to be worn as what we referred to in the US Army as a "Swiss seat" rappel harness, used for mountain or any other kind of rappelling. I pondered their use for the upcoming Valle Blanche "ski trip." *Are we going to have to do some rappelling at some point?* I pondered. Rather than ask Gilles a dumb and embarrassing question as the American officer in the group, I decided to ask Edwin.

"Edwin, what do we need these for?" I asked.

"In case you fall into a crevasse, there has to be some way of getting you out. Our guide carries extra rope. If he doesn't have enough rope, he can call for backup, and hopefully the damn thing is not so deep—or you are so hurt—that you can't be fished out of the crevasse," he said with a wink.

"*Great*, thanks for that beautiful image." I chuckled. "Nothing like being prepared for those pesky crevasses."

As we got on to the Aiguille du Midi cable car in Chamonix, at roughly 3,414 feet, we would take a twenty-minute ride on the longest single span cable car in the world, with a stop about midway for more passengers before the second leg of the cable car's climb, and finally ending up at the Aiguille du Midi peak, some 12,605 feet high. This also made the Aiguille du Midi (meaning "needle of the midday") cable car the highest vertical ascent of any cable car in the world.

As we got out of the cable car, I realized I must have had one cocktail too many the previous night: I was a bit lightheaded from the change in altitude. Once inside the main structure of the Aigulle du Midi peak, we had to take another elevator, which would take us several meters higher, to a veritable ice tunnel that led out to a narrow ridge, perhaps no more than six feet wide. On either side of the ridge were steep slopes descending into oblivion, with only a single strand rope, about waist high, to keep one from falling about 3,300 feet.

Just before leaving the tunnel, Gilles said, "Please stay directly behind me, on this trail and on the glacier, unless I tell you otherwise. If there are areas where we can free-ski, I will let you know. There are some areas like that, but they are dispersed throughout the trip." Not free-skiing meant we had to follow directly behind Gilles, like ducks in a row

We then started onto the ridge. In what seemed like the slowest—but certainly most focused—*shuffle* I had made in my life, after about forty to fifty meters, we were finally off the narrow ridge and onto a more open area. Here—thanks be to God—we would be able to get our skis on. The first test had been passed.

The first slope was icy but passable. As we descended it, I could see a deep crevasse about sixty feet off to my right. To my front lay an extended valley of white that slowly curved to the left and was surrounded with magnificent, partially snow-covered and rocky peaks. Not long after this, we got into a mogul field. But these were not the normal two- or three-feet-high moguls one might encounter at your typical ski resort in North America or Europe. These were more in the six- or seven-foot range. Some approached eight. You could stand on one side of a mogul and not see the person on the other side.

This is where I took my first fall. I got up as quickly as I could, as I did not want to slow the group down. With the huge moguls behind me, the second test was passed.

As we skied on in the morning through the *Mer del Glace* (Sea of Ice), we could see the *Requin Hut* farther below us. This would be our early lunch stop. But to get there, we had to traverse a fairly steep slope, single file, while just letting our skis run straight ahead, with no turns possible. Finally, we were within about 100 meters of the hut, which we then reached easily. Third test passed.

Lunch, taken on the sun-drenched patio, was enjoyable. But to be frank, it would have been more enjoyable were it at the end of what I now suspected would be one of the more physically challenging events of my life. Only US Army Ranger School, with its exhausting physical and mental challenges every day over fifty-six days, would end up being more physically challenging for this intermediate-level skier.

Pressing on after lunch, with no other skiers in sight, our guide, Gilles, would stop whenever he could to point out some of the most magnificent mountain peaks in the *Mont Blanc* range, several reaching 13,200 feet high. Some included *Aiguille Verte, Grandes Jorasses, Mont Blanc du Tacul,* and my unforgettable favorite because of its look and name, the *Dent du Geant* (the Tooth of the Giant). As we skied on, we would pass through the *Salle a Manger* (Dining Room) and Giant Icefall sections of the glacier. It was somewhere in these two areas where I faced my first real formidable challenge of the day, with the second soon to follow.

At a certain point, the six of us found ourselves in terrain that included a maze of roughly twenty-foot little hills, all interconnected. It was as if we had found world record-sized moguls. That in itself was not the major challenge, though. The challenge was that every one of them was coated in glare ice. Getting a ski edge to bite into the ice was extremely difficult, if not nigh impossible. Seeing that one person had already crashed and burned in front of me, I stood on top of one of these ice balls, gripped with—I ain't gonna lie—fear.

How in the world am I gonna ski off this massive ice ball without breaking my neck? I asked myself.

Standing there motionless, I was trying to think of what angle to the icy slope I should point my skis so they wouldn't get jammed up as soon as I hit the bottom of the slope, a slope that ended in a very constricted area, and that descended to a tight funnel formed by the icy upslope on the adjacent hill. All of a sudden, I heard this voice, whispered into my ear:

"Rick, you can *do* this."

It was the voice of Colonel Edwin Potocnik.

While I had been staring down that icy, constricted slope to figure out what my next move would be, Edwin had quietly made his way over to where I was standing. What he said was all I needed to hear. I immediately half-skied, half-slid down the slope to its constricted bottom. I was very relieved to somehow still be on my skis when I stopped. From there, I picked my next target to ski to.

Not long after, about five hours into our journey, we came to what would be a physical challenge for all of us. At some point, we had to make a hard-left turn so we could link up with the final long ski trail—perhaps three to four miles (roughly five to six kilometers)— which would take us back to the town of Chamonix. Whether we had overshot our turn or if there was simply no other choice because of how much the glacier had shifted, at one point we were forced to take off our skis and climb, in ski boots, a very steep slope of about 200 to 250 yards. I think most skiers will agree that hard plastic ski boots are challenging enough to walk in, let alone to climb, and to steeply climb at that.

With each and every step, we first had to get a firm toe hold in the snow and slippery slope, and then push straight up, while constantly leaning forward. Leaning backwards on the steep slope would have meant a long fall, requiring a repeat of the long, arduous climb, or worse. Additionally, all but one of us had to carry our ski poles in one hand and skis in another, which we tried to convert into crude and rather heavy walking sticks.

We were all quite envious of our Czech colleague, Major Ales Klepek. Klepek must have gotten some previous intelligence about this part of the Valle Blanche, as he had a special rucksack on which he could vertically strap a ski to each side. Instead of carrying two poles in one hand and two skis in the other like the rest of us, he could now use just his ski poles, one in each hand, as perfectly good stabilizers for climbing the steep slope.

About two-thirds of the way up the slope, due to the physical exertion of the steep climb while carrying skis and poles, I realized I had broken out into a total sweat, from head to toe. I even had sweat pooling in my ski boots. Fortunately, when we reached the top, there was a bench to take a break on and offer some relief for my shaky legs. The guide, as physically fit as he was, also insisted we take about a twenty-minute break. The fifth and final test of the approximately twenty-kilometer (twelve-mile) journey on the icy, crevasse-pocked glacier was essentially complete. Now it was just a matter of following the long but relatively easy trail back to Chamonix, where a well-earned beer awaited each of us.

CHAPTER 29

PURPLE HAZE

EVERY MILITARY COMMANDER NEEDS A strong executive officer or deputy commander to be effective. So, too, do ambassadors need strong deputies to help run their embassies and associated missions, while they are leading major diplomatic efforts, on behalf of the president, secretary of state and American people. In US diplomatic parlance, this deputy to the ambassador is referred to as the deputy chief of mission, or "DCM" (although we proliferate them, the US military is not the only organization with its fair share of acronyms). When he or she is running an embassy in the absence of an ambassador, they are referred to as the *chargé d'affairs* or just chargé for short.

At US Embassy Paris, the DCM is typically a highly experienced, top-flight diplomat who either has already been an ambassador at a smaller embassy or is about to become one. Alex Wolfe was such a DCM, so in February 2004, when he asked me to come to his office to talk about the June 2004 sixtieth anniversary of D-Day ceremonies, I took notice.

Within a very short time of our meeting in his office, adjacent to the ambassador's office, we got down to business.

"Rick, the ambassador and I have discussed it, and we think that you are a great choice to serve as the embassy's chairman for the Sixtieth Anniversary of D-Day ceremonies. As you know, the embassy normally plays a prominent role in the ceremonies, and, of course, Ambassador Leach and I want to make sure they are a big success. We think you have the leadership skills required for the job, and we'd like you to give it some serious thought. We do hope you accept," said Wolfe.

I noticed his statement was not exactly conditional. He did not say, "Rick, *you'd be* a great choice." He said, "You *are* a great choice." Alex's tone had an ever so slight *fait accompli* tone to it, so I would not take long in making my decision. It was all but formally made the instant after he mentioned it.

I was at once honored and challenged by the offer, knowing this was an event that only came around every ten years. I also knew that no defense attaché had been given the mantle of embassy leadership for it in the past. It had always been run by one or two of the senior foreign service officers in the embassy. I also considered Alex's—as well as Leach's—"offer" a vote of trust, one I certainly would not shun.

"Alex, I'm honored that you'd think of me for this responsibility," I responded. "I'd be happy to do it."

As I walked out of his office, I was feeling stimulated by the challenge, but also somewhat anxious. I knew this would be a major and high-profile planning, organizational, coordination, and execution event for 2004, for which exactly zero guidance or past best practices had been provided by anybody, including the State Department, Department of Defense, or US Embassy Paris.

Meanwhile, the US "punish France" approach, while it had abated, was still the elephant in the room. We in the DAO—and the entire embassy, for that matter—were operating off a blank screen when it came to planning for the Sixtieth Anniversary of D-Day ceremonies. With no clear vision or guidance from Washington, I joked about being in a "purple haze." I knew I had to change that in fairly short order.

One thing the Army professional military education system does a good job of imparting to commissioned officers is the "military decision-making process." Broadly, among other things, it is a method to analyze what is required—people, resources, time, etc.—for accomplishing a given mission. As I gathered a few DAO teammates—Lieutenant Colonel Cosby, Lieutenant Colonel Peterson, Colonel Jeff Jackson, and Commander Harold E. Williams (our outstanding naval attaché, Captain Deak Childress, was retiring to Virginia, to be replaced by Captain Mike Durnan, another exceptional naval officer, who would get accredited a couple of days before the ceremonies)—I realized we had very little experience, if any, running such an event of this scale and political magnitude.

We did have some experience, however, on a far smaller scale, resulting from a ceremony involving President Bush and conducted at the Omaha Beach cemetery over Memorial Day weekend in 2002 (four months before I arrived at the embassy). That would be a small-replica starting point, but we needed a lot more expertise, particularly for a visit involving the president of the United States, to ensure success.

I considered the challenges. There were many, including the support required for hosting of a presidential visit; the return of potentially several hundred D-Day and World War II veterans to France, and coordinating this entire, massive affair with our French colleagues, whom the Bush administration had spent most of 2003 trying to "punish" for their "failure" to support the United States-led war in Iraq. The President's visit, of course, ranked high on our list of reasons to get this right. However, it was the returning US veterans, many of whom had not set foot on French soil in roughly sixty years, as well as their accompanying family members, who were the "stars of the show." They were the ones for whom we most wanted to get this right.

Also high on the list of priorities were our relations with our French colleagues. We did not want them to deteriorate, in spite of some residual US "punish France" sentiments. The major challenges,

I was fairly confident our DAO team could manage, with the close cooperation, effort, and support of our embassy colleagues, the returning US veterans, and the on-the-ground coordination with French officials. It was the visit by the President of the United States, often referred to as POTUS, where we had the biggest blind spot in experience. I knew we had to do something about that, so about a week after our initial chat, I went back to Wolfe.

"Alex, I think we really need help with the presidential visit," I said. "We do lack experience on the logistics side, but I think we can overcome that in working with some of the experienced French and US hands in the embassy management office and elsewhere. But in the DAO, we are very much devoid of experience when it comes to a presidential visit and everything that portends," I added. "The State Department, on the other hand, deals with presidential visits every third month or so, or so it seems."

I knew that last statement was a bit of an exaggeration, but I also thought Alex would connect with my point. Fortunately, he did.

"I understand where you are coming from, Rick," said the US Embassy's number two person in charge. "What do you propose?"

"Alex, what I think we need is an embassy co-chair, from the State Department . . . a foreign service officer," I said. "Someone respected, who has had some experience with a presidential visit, or at least who knows which offices should be covering down on which tasks for such a visit."

Not only was I concerned about knowing exactly nothing about a US presidential visit, I was also concerned about having zero authority over the non-DAO personnel in the embassy: the management, logistics, protocol, public affairs, security, and contracting professionals, for example. A major portion of the embassy team would need to be involved to make this a success. One of their own, someone fairly senior, would be a great help in forming and leading an effective, embassy-wide team, for the optical effect, if nothing else.

A few days later, Wolfe and I met again.

"Rick, the ambassador agreed with your proposal concerning a co-chair," he said. "The individual we selected is Ken Merten."

"I know Ken," I said. "I think he is an excellent choice. Thanks for selecting someone I think will be a great fit."

I was very pleased that Merten got the nod to be the co-lead with me in planning, organizing, and executing what was widely believed would be the last major hurrah for the Greatest Generation veterans of the D-Day liberation of Europe. Ken was the deputy minister-counselor for US Embassy Paris's economics section. He was widely thought of as a competent, even-keeled, and steady leader, as well as a superb diplomat. Over the next few months we would make a great team. Ken would later go on to serve as ambassador to Haiti (during the horrific earthquake of 2010), as well as acting ambassador to Croatia.

As February turned into March 2004, I was quite concerned, as there had been absolutely zero involvement, or guidance, from the U.S Department of Defense concerning the Sixtieth D-Day Anniversary ceremonies, a major international event that was only three months away. Was this because of a lingering "punish France" attitude in the DoD? I wasn't sure, but it really didn't matter much because my DAO team needed to be busy doing as much preparatory work as we could, in spite of the information vacuum from the Pentagon. We would plan, ask questions, and begin to coordinate as much as we could, given the circumstances. If the DoD did finally chime in with some guidance, we would adjust accordingly.

Many of the bigger questions remained to be answered. Where would the epicenter of the event be? Omaha Beach? Utah Beach? Or *Pointe-du-Hoc*, where, in 1984, at the fortieth D-Day anniversary, President Ronald Reagan had given a masterful and memorable speech about the *Boys of Pointe-du-Hoc*, the heroic Army Rangers who scaled the ten-story cliffs there? Climbing sheer cliffs while hanging on to nothing but rope was daunting enough, but the Rangers did so in the face—and I do mean *in the face*—of deadly

German bullets raining on them from several yards above. At a great cost in casualties, these brave (words like "brave" just don't seem adequate sometimes) men eventually scaled those daunting cliffs. Once they did, they knocked out some of the artillery guns that had been massacring their fellow Americans on the beaches below.

On the greater US Embassy side of the ledger, we began holding meetings, if for nothing else than to make sure we were asking the right questions. For example, how much advance time was needed for reserving hotels in Normandy for hundreds of event organizers, veterans, and VIPs? Who, specifically, on the French side would be in charge of traffic? What in the way of support might the soldiers of US Army Europe be able to provide? Who should receive official invitations to the big event? What the heck *was* the big event? Would there be a flyover? How many veterans, and their family escorts, did we think might return? What about medical support for the mostly eighty-something-year-old veterans? It was an exhaustive list of issues that needed answering.

Thank goodness there were so-called *local nationals*, local French citizens who served at the US embassy, who were able to provide some institutional memory, as well as a handful of foreign service officers who had actually been assigned to the embassy for the fortieth or fiftieth anniversary events and were now back at US Embassy Paris.

In the meantime, my DAO team, which was at the heart of the planning for the event, began to develop contingencies. For example, if it was decided that the main venue would be at Utah Beach, we would follow Plan A. If it was at Omaha Beach, it would look like Plan B. If it involved a US-French parachute jump, it would look like Plan C, and so forth.

Meanwhile, in addition to whatever the US-centric celebration would be, farther north in the British sector at Arromanches, the scene of D-Day's Gold Beach operations and the "mulberry" false harbor that was built there, the French were planning a major international commemoration involving several heads of state. This would eventually include a controversial invitation by the French government to German Chancellor Gerhard Schroeder, who would be the first German head of state to attend a D-Day commemoration.

The Arromanches ceremony would also include President George W. Bush, as well as Prime Minister Tony Blair of Britain, Queen Elizabeth II, Russian President Vladimir Putin, Canadian Prime Minister Paul Martin, Australian Prime Minister John Howard, and the heads of state of Belgium, Norway, New Zealand, and the Netherlands. Just coordinating the arrival of those heads of state alone was a planning and coordination Rubik's cube.

As we got into late March, now less than ten weeks out, I finally received some information that eased my mind about the ceremony—*ceremonies*, actually, as there would be several. Army Lieutenant General (Ret.) Harry Edward "Ed" Soyster would be coming from the Pentagon to see me about the upcoming D-Day ceremonies. I'd heard Soyster's name before. I vaguely recalled receiving from him one of those congratulatory letters one gets from senior generals, with red stars on the letterhead, when I'd gotten promoted to major several years prior.

I was happy when the appointed day to meet Soyster in early April 2004 had arrived. As Acting Secretary of the Army Romer Leslie Brownlee's Special Assistant, Soyster had traveled from Washington D.C. to Paris on behalf of the secretary. I was expecting him to provide some significant guidance for the sixtieth D-Day anniversary ceremonies. In the meantime, I had prepared a briefing to bring him up to speed on the planning and contingency work that my DAO team, along with our embassy colleagues, had accomplished in preparing for these major D-Day ceremonies involving thousands of people.

PowerPoint has been used by the US Army for years, so it's possibly the height of Army heresy to say this, but—I was not a fan of it. I found the Army's reliance on it way overdone. The main objective seemed to be the slides themselves rather than truly effective planning, coordination, and execution. I thought the time spent on putting fancy pictures, having things fly in and out of the PowerPoint screen, and building multi-color "bubble charts," took away time from critical thinking, serious reflection, and other more pressing matters. Admittedly, I was "PowerPoint-impaired," but in short, I thought we spent entirely too much time on "showing" and not enough time "doing" or "preparing to do."

Nonetheless, in its simplest communicative and organizational form, PowerPoint *can* present a narrative, analysis, or plan efficiently. For Soyster, I would use a simple, black-and-white PowerPoint deskside briefing, held in a three-ring binder, to depict the spade work my team—along with embassy colleagues—had done prior to his arrival and in the absence of any tangible guidance from the Department of Defense.

"Sir, I'm glad to meet you, and I'm glad you're here," I said to Soyster as he entered the DAO spaces.

"Colonel Steinke, it's good to be here. I appreciate you taking the time to see me," the general said. He was dressed in civilian coat and tie.

After offering him a cup of coffee, I led him to my office coffee table, surrounded by a couch and some stuffed chairs. We exchanged a couple of pleasantries in a relaxed atmosphere induced almost entirely by General Soyster's easygoing demeanor.

Then I said, "Sir, if you don't mind, I'm going to bring you up to speed as to where we are regarding our efforts in getting ready for the big event in June."

"Rick, I'm very much looking forward to hearing about it," he said.

"Sir, do you have any guidance or anything you need to tell me up front, or anything in particular I should focus on before I get started?"

"No, Rick, I don't. Let's see what you have to say, and then we'll take it from there."

"That sounds like a plan, sir."

With that, I began the briefing with some assumptions, discussing what I *knew* to be true and concluding with what I thought were major issues still to be answered. During the briefing I discussed how the DAO-Embassy team was beginning to form, with the right embassy offices, and officers, identified for the right tasks. I told him we might get soldiers from US Army, Europe (USAREUR) to help us with the setup, administration, logistics, and security of the venue, *wherever* it might be, but USAREUR's participation was still to be confirmed. I told him what I knew about the macro issues for the event, such as the involvement of the French prefects in the overall security for Normandy and the gendarmes in securing the roads for the VIPs.

I also told him a few detailed and specific things for the event. For example, while he had not yet officially been named, I had a master of ceremonies in mind. He was the same master of ceremonies used for the fiftieth anniversary of D-Day ceremonies: Sergeant Major (Ret.) Dave Stewart, a Canadian-born American and US Army cavalry soldier who had eventually served with the Armed Forces Network (AFN) as a radio announcer. He was currently serving with Headquarters, US Army, Europe as a civilian public affairs officer. He was also a friend of my late father, US Army Sergeant First Class Harvey F. Steinke, who had died in 1995. I trusted Stewart completely, and knew there was nobody else on the planet who could do a better job.

Toward the end of the thirty-minute briefing, I informed Soyster that my biggest concern was that we did not have a designated venue yet. Would it be Omaha Beach? More specifically, would it be the Normandy American Cemetery and Memorial at Colleville-sur-Mer? Would it be Utah Beach? Pointe-du-Hoc? Somewhere else? When I concluded my briefing, I was ready to hear his concerns and receive his guidance.

"Rick, let me begin by saying this is the first indication I have received that someone in Paris is seriously thinking about, planning for, and even troubleshooting this big event, particularly given the lack of guidance you have received from the Pentagon. Furthermore, you have just provided me a serious boost in confidence that we are actually going to have a great ceremony," said Lieutenant General Soyster.

"Thank you, sir, I appreciate the feedback," I said. "I also realize we are just getting started in terms of work to be done."

"Well, you are certainly off to a great start. Now, let me tell you about a few things that should help clear up the rather hazy picture you are having to deal with. First of all, US Army Europe will indeed be providing support to the event," said General Soyster. "They may have already been given the mission, and if they haven't already been notified, they will be imminently."

"Sir, that is a key piece of intel."

"Secondly, and perhaps most importantly, it's the White House that will be in the driver's seat for this event. Events like these, which include a presidential visit, are normally run out of the White House Chief of Staff's office," said Soyster. "I would expect you'll be hearing about a venue within two to three weeks at the most, and after that, things will move quite quickly."

"That is new and valuable information as well."

"So overall, Rick, the upfront analysis, planning, and coordination your team has done will provide huge benefits for laying down a base of US embassy support for the overall effort. Now it's really more a matter of tweaking . . . okay, perhaps tweaking is too mild of a word. Let me say, *adapting* the plan. This will be a great event. I am now sure of it."

Soyster and I also talked about other aspects of the big event, but I, too, now had some degree of confidence that, in spite of not knowing exactly where the main venue would be, our DAO-Embassy team was on the right track. Our attitude and collective morale were good, too, which I believed was key to making this a memorable event for, above all, the returning D-Day heroes and their accompanying families.

CHAPTER 30

WHITE HOUSE PRE-ADVANCE TEAM

WITHIN DAYS OF LIEUTENANT GENERAL Ed Soyster's brief but productive visit, I received a phone call from Deputy Chief of Mission Alex Wolfe.

"Rick, I just got off the phone with the White House," said Wolfe. "They will be bringing a pre-advance team to France next week to begin the on-the-ground preparations for the Sixtieth D-Day Anniversary events. I want to make sure you stay closely linked up with them during their visit. I expect they'll be with us for about three days," he said.

"Thank you for the heads-up, Alex," I responded. "Did they say if they have selected a venue yet?"

"They said they had not yet decided, and that one significant reason for the trip was to do just that."

"Alex, thanks again for the call. I look forward to the visit," I said.

Now well into April, and roughly eight weeks away from the big event, I was very thankful that we would soon be getting some clarification on the specifics of where and how the event would flow. The great majority of the work for pulling off a world-class event was still to be done. This included organizing the venue itself; arranging and contracting for transportation and lodging for veterans, guests, government officials, and VIPs; sending out invitations; determining side events, such as a bilateral meeting between the two heads of state, US President George W. Bush and French President Jacques Chirac; and coordinating the timing of the US affair with the big international event in Arromanches, involving several heads of state. Given that the air of the US "punish France" approach to US-France relations still lingered, I pondered how the White House pre-advance visit would go.

Although serving as a US Army foreign area officer in the defense attaché position, I was now thankful that I'd had previous extensive experience as a battalion and brigade plans, operations, and training officer (S-3). I had served three times in this role, once for an Italian mountain infantry ("Alpini") battalion, and subsequently for a US field artillery battalion, and a third time as a brigade S-3 for a field artillery brigade, consisting of three field artillery battalions, as many different weapons systems and about 2,000 artillerymen. In all, I had served almost five years as an S-3 plans, operations, and training officer. These assignments, in addition to serving as a field artillery battalion commander, provided valuable operational experiences for planning, coordinating, and executing large operations involving hundreds, and sometimes thousands of people with several moving parts.

In addition to the very welcome news that the White House was sending a pre-advance team to France to prepare the big June 5 and 6 events, I also got word that US Army, Europe (USAREUR) had now officially received the mission to support the US sixtieth anniversary of D-Day events. Whether that was due to Soyster's prodding, I cannot be sure, but the timing of our meeting and the subsequent USAREUR notification would certainly seem to suggest it. In any case, my two assistant Army attachés, Lieutenant Colonel Bill Cosby and newly promoted Lieutenant Colonel Eric Peterson, immediately reached out to appropriate USAREUR staff officers to begin to effect coordination about the event, wherever it might be held.

In the meantime, a retired Army major who worked in the embassy's regional security office (RSO) informed me I needed to spend some time with the French prefect of a place where some part of the events would be held, either the Basse Normandy region or the specific Calvados district (time, as well as some alcohol consumed with said prefect, has dimmed my memory a bit). This was true no matter where the final specific venue would be.

The major informed me that the presidential visit to Normandy and Normandy American Cemetery at Colleville-sur-Mer for Memorial Day 2002, had resulted in a fistfight between some members of the US Secret Service and their French counterparts. The prefect, who would essentially be in charge for things like traffic control and overall, on-the-ground security for the D-Day events, was apparently not amused. He contended it was the US Secret Service that was out of line and had started the entire melee where, apparently, some people got hurt.

What the major suggested was that I have dinner with and make amends with—in effect, "butter up"—the prefect, who apparently held a grudge against the Secret Service and government officials writ large from the May 2002 dustup. I agreed. The major eventually got back to me and informed me that a dinner had been arranged at a chateau in the Normandy countryside.

On the appointed evening, I attended a dinner with the prefect and eight other people present, roughly split between his office and the US Embassy. He was a few years my elder, but fortunately, we hit it off. The prefect responded positively to my olive branch, although I never said or hinted at a *colpa nostra* admission to starting the fight. Frankly, I had no idea how the fisticuffs got started. The details of what the prefect and I discussed are a bit hazy, as he loved red wine (which is pretty much part of the French DNA), and I endeavored to make sure we would share this in common during our dinner.

What I do recall, however, is that the chateau's courtyard had been the actual scene of the dustup between the US and French Secret

Service members, making the dinner's location all the more relevant. I kept conversation as light as possible, usually deferring to him to lead. In the end, after having what was probably a drink too many for my country, the prefect and I amicably parted ways. After that, we never had an issue jointly coordinating the security, traffic, and major transportation means—planes, trains, buses, and automobiles—for the ceremonies.

Meanwhile, the White House team was set to arrive at US Embassy Paris. Led by deputy chief of staff Joe Hagin, who was in his forties, most of his entourage would be in their thirties, and even twenties. A dynamic and energetic group, many of whom were volunteers, they each brought different reasons and talents for being on the team. Some were there to develop choreography, others to get the right pictures or media coverage, others had an eye toward security. Still others were looking to enhance the president's speech to be delivered at the venue, with locally acquired stories or facts. The bottom line was that this group got things done, quickly if needed. When you speak for the White House, things tend to happen that way, as I was soon to learn.

I found Hagin an even-keeled, in-charge, and confident but not cocky leader of the group. He was very mission-focused.

"Rick, there are a few places I'd like to take a close look at," he said at our first meeting. "They include Utah Beach, Omaha Beach, and Pointe-du-Hoc, unless you'd like to recommend any others."

"No, sir, I think those are the main venues that deserve serious consideration," I replied. "How do you plan on visiting those locations? Should I meet you there?"

"Actually, what I'd like is that you ride with us on the bus as we visit each site," he said.

"It will be my pleasure, sir."

Accordingly, the pre-advance team visited each major venue by bus, with Hagin and me riding up front. The first stop was at Utah Beach. At this location, we were met by the local mayor of Carentan, members of the American Battle Monuments Commission, French gendarmes, a local representative or two of the French parliament, and other local French government officials. While Utah Beach was still in Normandy, it was in a different department than Omaha Beach. Here, we would meet officials from the Manche department (versus the Calvados department for Omaha Beach). We were already able to sense a bit of rivalry between the Utah Beach political and economic promoters and those of Omaha Beach.

As Hagin walked the ground with the senior political representatives, he got a pretty good earful as to why Utah Beach would be the best choice as the main venue for the ceremonies. Of course, the Utah Beach affiliates would have a ceremony nonetheless, but by being the main venue, they would host not only the bulk of returning veterans, but the American and French heads of state, and the thousands of visitors who would throng to see them. Meanwhile, subject matter experts on the White House pre-advance team surveyed the area for a host of suitability criteria.

A very similar scene played out at Normandy American Cemetery, which overlooked Omaha Beach and was near the town of Colleville-sur-Mer. The Pointe-du-Hoc venue, however, did not have the kind of local political representation that the Normandy American Cemetery and Utah Beach locations did. I assessed this as mainly due to the fact that Pointe-du-Hoc was more physically remote than the Omaha Beach and Utah Beach sites.

Leaving the area, the next day, I thought that the Normandy American Cemetery was probably the favorite to be selected. The cemetery itself, with its perfectly aligned sea of marble crosses, was a poignant venue that the other two locations did not have. Although the Pointe-du-Hoc Army Rangers had a hell of a fight on their hands and took significant losses to their 200-plus man force, "bloody Omaha" was where the heaviest fighting—and great heroism— took place. At one point the situation became so dire that US Army General Omar Bradley had considered evacuating the entire force off the beach. Furthermore, topping President Ronald Reagan's 1984 historic and highly lauded *The Boys of Pointe du Hoc* speech would have been a serious challenge to even the best of presidential orators.

Utah Beach units also met deadly resistance, but not with the same intensity and duration as those units at Pointe-du-Hoc and Omaha Beach. The main Utah Beach units, such as the US 4th, 9th, and 90th divisions, did not face the same volume of enemy fire that the US 29th and 1st Infantry Divisions did at Omaha Beach, for example. This was due to several factors. One was the more effective pre-allied bombing and the early-morning, behind-the-lines airborne drops by the 82nd and 101st Airborne Divisions behind Utah Beach. Both airborne divisions fought multiple hellish and valiant local battles, and significantly disrupted German defenses in the Normandy countryside, thus taking much of the pressure off Utah Beach.

To be fair, however, one must recall that *all* units in the immediate days, weeks, and months after they got ashore—the 4th, 9th, and 90th Infantry Divisions included—still had eleven months of ferocious combat they would have to face against the German Wehrmacht. In fact, it wouldn't be until early August 1944, some nine to ten weeks after D-Day, that US and allied forces would finally break out of the Normandy cauldron. Furthermore, the focus for the D-Day (called "Jour J" by the French) ceremonies was, well, D-Day, so I believed that slightly favored Omaha Beach as the primary venue.

So, apparently, did the White House. That was the venue, centered around the Normandy American Cemetery and Memorial at Colleville-sur-Mer, the site of 9,387 buried American heroes, where the sixtieth anniversary of D-Day ceremonies would be focused.

There was, however, not one area that was more sacred than others—all of these beaches were holy ground.

CHAPTER 31

WHITE HOUSE ADVANCE TEAM TAKES CHARGE

APPROXIMATELY ONE WEEK BEFORE THE June 5–6 sixtieth anniversary of D-Day ceremonies, the area in and around the Normandy American Cemetery at Colleville-sur-Mer was a flurry of activity and people. US Army Europe had provided Major General David T. Zabecki, a Vietnam War infantry rifleman, as USAREUR's senior representative to the event. USAREUR also provided a contingent of several hundred US Army soldiers, housed in tents in a temporary base camp adjacent to the cemetery, to support the event. The USAREUR soldiers were ably led by an energetic and enthusiastic military police brigade commander, Colonel James B. Brown.

The White House advance team was back, too, only this time with greater numbers and intensity, led by a thirty-something Mike Heath, the senior advance representative for the White House. My job was to support the advance team on a wide range of issues, to include US Embassy support, working with US Army Europe, interpreting English and French when required, and liaising with the French Armed Forces.

Each day consisted of coordinating, preparing, and, toward the end of the week, rehearsing. Rehearsal included every choreographed detail, from who would arrive when, who would greet whom, who would sit where, when the master of ceremonies would start, where the press would be located, how traffic control for the VIPs and returning US veterans would work, how traffic control for the public would work, parking issues, medical support, protocol challenges, and what actions the two heads of state, President George W. Bush and President Jacques Chirac, would take and when. It was a fairly complex operation, but one for which we were fortunately now very well-resourced.

Each evening, a group of about eight to ten of us would meet around 9:00 p.m. at the Le Sapiniere restaurant, located directly on Omaha Beach, to go over the yet-to-be-resolved issues of the day, and to prepare for the next day's activities. Given the six-hour time difference with the White House, this would also provide an opportunity for Mike Heath and other advance team members to call back for clarification, decisions, or guidance on any outstanding issues.

One of those issues was the responsibility of Scott Sforza, the deputy assistant to the president for communications and production. It was how to get the best possible ceremony photograph of the two heads of state, particularly President Bush. Scott was the former senior producer for a popular and fast-paced American television political talk show called *The McLaughlin Group* as well as *John McLaughlin's One on One*. Scott had also been the director of television communications for the successful Bush-Cheney 2000 presidential campaign.

"Rick, it's all about 'the shot,'" Scott told me. "This will be *the* photograph that will be sent around the world to show President Bush's presence, in the best possible light, at these ceremonies." Less than three days before the start of the biggest D-Day ceremonies ever, I would learn just how important "the shot" was, and just how much capacity the White House advance team had for getting things done quickly. As it was turning out, the Omaha Beach cemetery and memorial layout were not very conducive to getting "the shot."

The main issue involved how best to photograph President Bush, accompanied by President Chirac, as he walked from laying the wreath at the cemetery's center-piece memorial and bronze statue, *Spirit of American Youth Rising from the Waves*, to the podium and the over 700 waiting D-Day veterans and their family members. Given the layout of the podium and the seating for US veterans, VIPs, and the attending public (some 6,000-plus in all), both heads of state would have to walk around a major obstacle: the approximately sixty-meter-long and thirty-meter-wide basin in the foreground of the memorial.

"No problem," said Scott Sforza. "We'll have a bridge built, or at least that will be my recommendation." *Did he just say that?* I asked myself, thinking Scott might be half-joking.

"Are you serious, Scott?" I asked. "Do you think that's possible, given that we are less than three days from showtime? I mean, we essentially only have two full days left to prepare."

"Oh, it's definitely possible, and moreover, it's very doable. It will produce the exact photo we're looking for."

I went to bed that evening highly intrigued and curious as to what the last two preparation days before the "big day" would bring.

On the following morning, I arrived at the Normandy American Cemetery a bit earlier than I had on most days, having concluded meetings with the White House advance team at around 11:00 p.m. the night prior. When I arrived at the cemetery around 7:30 a.m., one of my assistant Army Attachés, Lieutenant Colonel Bill Cosby, informed me we had a problem.

"Sir, it seems one of our close-in and key designated parking areas for the day after tomorrow's ceremony has been blocked," said Bill Cosby.

"What do you mean 'blocked?'" I asked.

"Well, it seems a big cement barricade has been towed in to block the entrance. I understand this was done by the (local) Colleville-sur-Mer mayor, who is not happy about where his seat is located for Sunday's ceremony. It seems he thinks he should be much higher on the protocol list."

"Thanks for the heads-up, Bill. I'm going to go out there with Thierry and have a look for myself," I answered. Thierry was my driver. "In the meantime, please confirm that it was the mayor who did this."

Within about fifteen minutes of our conversation, I had arrived at the large field, located a short driving distance from the cemetery. It had been converted to a parking lot for the D-Day ceremonies. As one might imagine, the parking and traffic plans, not to mention the timing of the presidential planes and helicopters arriving in the area, involved meticulous planning and coordination for an event including tens of VIPs, hundreds of returning US veterans, two heads of state, many congressional and government leaders, and thousands of attendees. In fact, the main public transportation plan involved shutting down entire highways and roads within thirty miles (or fifty kilometers) of the cemetery, as well as a public parking and busing plan that began about the same distance away. Therefore, relatively close parking was at a premium, reserved only for select VIPs and groups.

As I arrived at the designated VIP parking area, sure enough, there was a solid cement barricade—about five meters across and a meter high—at the entrance. After verifying that this had indeed been directed by the Colleville-sur-Mer mayor, I pondered what to do. I thought about whether I should appeal on his behalf for a better seat at the event. But then again, I thought this was such a low-class move that I wouldn't bother. I wasn't really interested in rewarding his poor judgment.

I also realized I had no power to *compel* the mayor to remove it. But I knew someone who did. Someone with whom I had developed a warm personal relationship since my arrival in France, and who had offered to help if I ever got in a jam. That someone was French Colonel (Ret.) Charlie Deleris, the personal advisor to France's chief of defense, General Henri Bentégeat. He was the same Deleris who had introduced himself to me my first time at the Ecole Militaire with General Jim Jones. Since then, we had developed an excellent working relationship, and quite a friendly personal one. While staring at that annoying cement barrier, I called him.

"Charlie, this is Rick Steinke," I said.

"Rick, how are you, buddy?" he asked. "How are things going at Normandy? The big day is right around the corner!"

"Yep, Charlie, it sure is," I replied. "Which is why I'm calling you. Seems the mayor of Colleville-sur-Mer isn't really happy about where he is on the protocol pecking order for the ceremony and has decided to block a key parking area next to the venue as a result," I said. "I thought you might perhaps know a way that we would get him to change his mind about that barrier."

"What? Are you *kidding* me?" responded Deleris. "Don't worry, Rick, we'll get him to remove that thing within a few hours. I'll just need a little time to call a couple of folks on behalf of General Bentégeat."

"Charlie, I'm deeply indebted," I replied.

"Rick, don't give it a second thought."

As I returned to the Normandy American Cemetery, where much activity and rehearsals were taking place, I noticed a big white truck, almost the size of a semi-trailer, from a commercial company in Belgium. It was parked next to the main water basin that was precluding "the shot" of President Bush. From the back of the truck, a husky man was beginning to offload iron tubes of varying lengths, the type used for industrial-grade scaffolding. The scaffolding was the kind that's used for building or restoring multi-story buildings or structures.

Within a couple of hours, I was beginning to see the outline of a structure—a bridge, by golly—that would span the length of the entire reflective basin, with a height of about one and a half to two meters, or about four to six feet, above the water. Eventually, it would support a walkway, perhaps three meters (or ten feet) wide. On that walkway would eventually appear a red carpet, perfect for the two most powerful men in the United States and France, to walk on. Scott Sforza would have his bridge. "The shot" would be produced.

Around 6:00 p.m., with only one full day left before the Normandy American Cemetery would begin to be abuzz with activity, I thought I'd double-check to make sure the cement barrier had been pulled out of the way of my VIP parking area. I was more than happy to find that it had not only been pulled out of the way, it was nowhere to be seen.

The next morning, on June 5, 2004, I had to return to Paris for a major event to be held in the stone courtyard of Les Invalides. The French government had invited 100 US veterans, along with three Australians, to return to France to receive the French Legion of Honor (full name: National Order of the Legion of Honor). The 100 selected had gone through a fairly rigorous process (testing, among other things, whether the mostly octogenarian veterans were fit for long-distance travel) conducted by the US Department of Veteran's Affairs (VA). The VA ensured the selectees represented a wide swath of D-Day soldiers. This included doctors, nurses, sailors, and pilots.

One of the pilots was former US presidential candidate and senator (1963-1981) from South Dakota, George McGovern. McGovern had flown thirty-five combat missions over North Africa and Italy. He was awarded America's second highest military medal, the Distinguished Flying Cross, for piloting his damaged bomber across Yugoslavia to a remote island runway. That runway was shorter than was required to land safely. To make the landing, McGovern had his crew threw all their non-essential equipment overboard, and both he and his co-pilot stood on the brake as it was touching down.

First established in 1802 by Napoléon Bonaparte, the *Légion d'Honneur* is France's highest order of merit for military and civil merits. In addition to the US and Australian veterans present, about thirty US Members of Congress were in attendance at the event as well. French Minister of Defense Michèle Alliot-Marie presided over the entire affair. Before each veteran received his award, a French officer declared:

"In the name of the president of the Republic and by virtue of the powers conferred on us, you are hereby named a chevalier (knight) of the Legion of Honor."

That night, on the eve of the sixtieth anniversary ceremonies, I arrived back at the local US Embassy operational headquarters that had been established at the local Omaha Beach Mercure Hotel. One of our US Embassy staffers stopped me in the Operations Room.

"Colonel Steinke, we had two gentlemen who just contacted us for help in getting a last-minute rental car," the embassy official said.

"Oh, really? What were their names?" I asked.

"Tom Hanks and Stephen Spielberg," came the reply.

"Well, I think we can arrange that," I said.

CHAPTER 32

D-DAY SIXTY YEARS LATER

AS I WENT TO MY room that evening of June 5 to join my family, who had traveled up to attend the next day's ceremonies, I mentioned Tom Hanks and Stephen Spielberg would be there.

"Dad, if you see Tom Hanks, you *have* to get his autograph," said twelve-year-old Erika. "Okay? Please?"

Not wanting to throw water on her enthusiasm, I agreed to do so.

"Sure, sweetie," I said. "If I see him, I will do it."

As the morning of June 6 finally arrived, I was a bit concerned my family would not be ready to depart the hotel at 7:00 a.m., when I needed to leave. But they were ready to go, including our youngest, six-year-old trooper, Maria. As we stepped outside, I was thankful that the weather was better than the miserable conditions those Greatest Generation soldiers had to endure sixty years before to the day. It was a magnificent and crisp morning with a bluebell sky.

Arriving at the cemetery at 0730, we beat the crowds by quite a bit, although many of the people involved in the ceremony were already beginning to arrive or set up. Once I got Susan, Erika, and Maria seated, I began to make a few last-minute checks to ensure all was well.

As the morning progressed, French President Jacque Chirac's helicopter was the first to land, before President Bush's. Not appointed as one of the main greeters, I kept my distance, standing perhaps ten meters (thirty-three feet) from the French president and the small group gathered around him, which included the Normandy American Cemetery Director. However, President Chirac's daughter, Laurence Chirac, apparently recognizing my US Army uniform, came up to me.

"Are you aware that several journalists are stuck at the cemetery's entry point? Do you think you could do something about that?" she asked in a pleasant tone.

"I was not aware of that, and I will get in touch with someone immediately," I responded.

US Army Colonel Jim Brown was the commander of the 18th military police brigade from Mannheim, Germany. By now I practically had him on speed dial. I called him, and the journalists were subsequently all allowed to enter the cemetery in fairly short order.

As the morning went on, I began to see several high-ranking members of the Bush administration making their way into the cemetery, including US Secretary of State Colin Powell. Secretary of Defense Donald Rumsfeld did not make it over, but the senior US military officer and chairman of the Joint Chiefs of Staff, General Richard Myers, did. We had a good chat right after the ceremony's conclusion and before I moved on to the afternoon international ceremony at Arromanches.

Several minutes before the start of the ceremony, Tom Hanks and Stephen Spielberg were standing no more than twenty feet from me, not far from what would soon be the president's podium. An Army sergeant, perhaps from the White House communications team or the military police brigade, went up to Mr. Hanks and got his autograph. All of a sudden, I felt a nudge from behind. I turned around, and it was French Minister of Defense Michèle Alliot-Marie's military aide-de-camp, Lieutenant Colonel Thierry Delavaud.

"Rick, go get Tom Hanks's autograph, and I will take a photo," he said.

"Thierry, I'm not sure, but—" I said, before he interrupted me.

"Go now, Rick, before the ceremony starts," he insisted.

While I knew I had made the promise to Erika, I was now feeling quite conflicted about asking. *Tom Hanks and Stephen Spielberg are here for the American heroes of D-day, not some desk-driving military attaché living in Paris,* I thought uncomfortably.

Nonetheless, I decided to do what I had promised.

I took a few steps forward and said, "Mr. Hanks, my daughter said if I saw you this morning, I had to get your autograph." Then I sheepishly added, "If you don't mind."

Very graciously, Hanks replied, "Well, we certainly don't want to disappoint your daughter, do we?" He signed the 3x5 card I happened to have in my breast pocket.

"Thank you, Captain Miller," I said, using his *Saving Private Ryan* character's name.

While I had kept a promise, I didn't feel great about bothering him for his autograph. He and Mr. Spielberg were doing a pretty good job of keeping a low profile, and it was clear they were there with only the best of intentions, that of acknowledging and respecting the American heroes of D-Day. Afterward, I also thought about how it was actors like Tom Hanks (in my opinion, one of the greatest ever) who draw the affinity and adulation of the American people, while right beside them are the magnificent directors and producers, such as Stephen Spielberg, who bring the best movies to life but receive less attention, at least from the public.

Within a few minutes, the ceremony began with the silver-throated master of ceremonies, US Army Sergeant Major (Ret.) Dave Stewart briefly addressing the audience. There were well over 6,000 people in attendance, mostly French citizens, in the folding chairs behind me, roughly the maximum number that the cemetery could reasonably hold. Most importantly, there were an estimated 700-plus

US D-Day veterans seated around Presidents Bush and Chirac as they addressed the crowd. A 21-artillery howitzer salute, directed by D-Day veterans, would start the ceremony.

As the two heads of state laid the wreath at the main memorial and then made their way to the water basin and walked across the red-carpeted, recently constructed bridge, I heard hundreds of cameras clicking away. I was confident Scott Sforza would have "the shot" he was looking for.

President Jacques Chirac was the first to speak, delivering heartfelt words to the US veterans and people present.

"France will never forget. She will never forget that 6th of June, 1944, the day hope was reborn and rekindled. She will never forget those men who made the ultimate sacrifice to liberate our soil, our native land, our continent from the yoke of Nazi barbarity and its murderous folly. Nor will it ever forget its debt to America, its everlasting friend, and to its allies—all of them—thanks to whom Europe, reunited at last, now lives in peace, freedom, and democracy . . .

"Here, on Omaha Beach, on bloody Omaha, today, as we stand in respectful silence, our emotion is undimmed at the spectacle of these rows upon rows of crosses, where your companions, your brothers-in-arms, fallen on the field of honor, now rest for all of eternity. Our hearts are indeed heavy as we contemplate their courage, their self-sacrifice, their generosity. And our spirit is indeed uplifted by the absolute ideals of these youngsters, who offered up their last breath to save the world."

Following President Chirac, President Bush's somewhat longer speech also resonated among the US veterans and French citizens present:

"History reminds us that France was America's first friend in the world. With us today are Americans who first saw this place at a distance, in the half-light of a Tuesday morning long ago. Time and providence have brought them back to see once more the beaches and the cliffs, the crosses and the Stars of David . . .

"All who are buried and named in this place are held in the loving memory of America. We pray in the peace of this cemetery that they have reached the far shore of God's mercy. And we still look with pride on the men of D-Day, on those who served and went on. It is a strange turn of history that called on young men from the prairie towns and city streets of America to cross an ocean and throw back the marching, mechanized evils of fascism. And those young men did it. *You* did it."

President Bush also acknowledged President Ronald Reagan, who had just died the day prior.

After he concluded his speech, he moved into the crowd, along with President Chirac, to shake the hands of the living American heroes of Normandy. I eventually saw US Air Force General and Chairman of the Joint Chiefs of Staff Richard Myers, whom it was my job to represent to his French counterpart, General Henri Bentégeat. We had a good chat for about fifteen minutes or so concerning US-France military-to-military relations, which were in excellent shape in spite of earlier "punish France" measures.

For example, roughly two to three months prior, US and French military forces had worked together restoring the peace in Haiti. Haiti had erupted in violence after its president, Jean Bertrand-Aristide, had fled under the pressure of a military uprising (some declared it a coup d'état) as well as at the behest of the Bush Administration. Under a so-called United Nations *Multinational Interim Force*, the US and France had worked closely together, with France eventually providing the largest continent of peacekeepers in Haiti, some 4,000 in all.

As the Normandy American Cemetery event concluded, the two heads of state, along with US Ambassador Howard Leach, departed by helicopter (Marine One) to the city of Caen, where a major international lunch was held, along with several other heads of state and senior government officials. I, instead, boarded a bus full of 29th Infantry Division veterans headed for the international ceremony to be held at Arromanches. Along the way, I had the honor and privilege of speaking extensively with two 29th Division veterans, both of the storied 116th Infantry Regiment, which waded into the hellish teeth of the Wehrmacht's defenses at dawn on June 6, 1944.

Before the D-Day operations were complete, among the roughly 4,413 dead allied soldiers (accounts vary), nineteen soldiers from one small town in America—Bedford, Virginia, population 3,000— would perish. All nineteen belonged to Company A, 1st Battalion, 116th Infantry Regiment, 29th Infantry Division. Three more young men from Bedford would die in Europe before the war's end. "The Bedford Boys" would forever represent the young men and women from across small-town America who made the ultimate sacrifice for the freedoms we all have today.

World War II veterans have an almost universal reputation for talking very little of the combat they endured. When they finally did talk, it was often in the twilight of their days on earth. Most just wanted to "return to the United States and get on with their lives," somehow burying the emotional and psychological trauma so many endured.

During the bus ride with the veterans of the 29th Division, I spoke with two members of the 116th Infantry Regiment: Mr. Van Cook, the regiment's artillery liaison officer at the time of the D-Day landings, and Mr. Earl Wilkinson, an infantry rifleman and squad leader. True to form, both soldiers were dismissive of the idea that they'd done anything special in the war. I sensed, however, that both possessed a remarkable resilience, keeping a sense of humor about the war and what they'd experienced.

Yet the 116th Infantry Regiment was one of the most heavily engaged units in World War II, fighting across France and through Germany until the war ended for the regiment at the Elbe River. From a regiment that started with roughly 3,000 men, from June 6, 1944, until V-E Day on May 8, 1945, the 116th Infantry Regiment suffered casualties of 1,298 killed, 4,769 wounded, and 594 missing for a total of 7,113. A continuous stateside individual replacement system was what kept the regiment fighting until war's end.

Both Cook and Wilkinson also noted the realism of the *Saving Private Ryan* movie.

"Yep, they got that one right," said Cook. "Many of us got quite seasick on the ride across the channel. Many men were practically beggin' to get off those boats, but, of course, few of us knew what was about to hit us," he said.

Mr. Wilkinson, who had led a squad of about ten men for much of the war, was also quite matter-of-fact and self-effacing.

"There were a lot who were not heroes," he said. "Some did not want to come out of their foxholes."

For me, his statement was yet another example of the humility of a US World War II veteran of that era, not wanting the accolades to be too great, lest they somehow exceed the tremendous commitment to duty and courage displayed by so many in that generation.

During the interludes of my privileged conversation with the two D-Day veterans of the 29th Division, I thought of my two wonderful French friends, Laurent Lefebvre and Sophie Lefebvre-Malherbe, who make it from Paris to their home in Normandy whenever they can.

There are those French, and they are legion, who hold the memories of the sacrifices of the D-Day liberators dear to their hearts, and who take the time to remember them on special occasions. They also ensure their children are schooled as to the events of the Normandy liberation. Then there are Laurent and Sophie, who are in an extra-special category of love and support for US World War II veterans. The two Paris police officers personally adopted the veterans of the "29 Let's Go!" Division as their own (and in several cases, vice-versa), organizing local cruises on the Seine River, doing fundraisers to bring 29th Division veterans to France, personally visiting 29th Division veterans and their families in the United States, publishing oral histories (e.g., *They Were on Omaha Beach: 194 Eyewitnesses,* 2003) and developing a website, www.americandday.org, that will be a magnificent treasure trove of D-Day information for generations to come.

Finally reaching Arromanches, farther up the Normandy coast and into what was the British sector for the D-Day landings, I said goodbye to my fellow travelers of the US 29th Infantry Division. To the degree I could get them to talk, I could have listened to them for hours.

As I got off the bus, I noticed that Arromanches, site of the international venue for the D-Day ceremonies, had a different feel than the Normandy American Cemetery. It was made primarily from multiple bleachers, set in a semi-oval fashion and facing out to the sea. Slightly below the bleachers was a large platform where international military bands and dancers would perform, with big video screens in the background. In front of the seating area, which held perhaps 3,500 attendees, were the places for the heads of state. This would be more of a spectacle than the solemn Normandy ceremony.

In fact, virtually all of the attending nations at Arromanches had held their national ceremonies that morning, followed by a lunch at the historic city hall in Caen. For example, Queen Elizabeth II, thanking Canadian soldiers who had come ashore on D-Day, had presided over the ceremony at Juno Beach. A similar ceremony was held at the British-French memorial in Bayeux, which also included Queen Elizabeth II, as well as President Chirac. Now, at the afternoon ceremony in Arromanches of the then-British sector, more than ten heads of state would gather, including Russian President Vladimir Putin and German Chancellor Gerhard Schroeder, a first for a German chancellor.

Two features stood out for me at that ceremony. The first was the arrival of President George W. Bush and First Lady Laura Bush. Prior to the official start of the event, the crowd had politely cheered each time the arrival of a head of state was announced. However, when President Bush's motorcade and limousine, with American flags fluttering in the afternoon breeze, approached the venue as the last head of state to arrive, the crowd reacted with an enthusiastic *roar* and loud applause. Even given all of the preceding US- "Old

Europe" rancor over the Iraq war, on this D-Day anniversary, this reaction seemed to define what it still meant to be the President of the United States of America: very much appreciated and respected.

The second feature, less prominent than the US President's arrival but memorable for me nonetheless, of the Arromanches D-Day ceremonies was the performance of His Majesty the Kings Guard Band and Drill Team of Norway. They positively stole the show.

As the ceremony concluded and I headed back to the Omaha Beach Mercure Hotel in Colleville-sur-Mer, I believed that these sixtieth D-Day ceremonies, particularly at Normandy, went as well as could have been expected. This was especially true given the late start we had planning and coordinating the event. In the end, the US veterans who returned with their families were well-appreciated, respected, and cared for. President Bush's visit, too, was a big success.

The ceremonies, jointly attended and honored by US, French, Canadian, and European allies, also finally turned the corner on the "punish France" policy. It seemed that remembering our common fight against our common enemy in WWII allowed us to renew our common friendship on the sixtieth anniversary of D-Day.

CHAPTER 33

THEOULE-SUR-MER

"COLONEL STEINKE, YOU HAVE A letter here from the mayor of Theoule-sur-Mer," said Becky Bouvier, my secretary. "He wants to invite you to come and participate in some ceremonies during the middle of August. He also mentions a speech and a few other things."

"Oh, really?" I asked. "Where is Theoule-sur-Mer?"

"It's on the French Riviera," she said. "Not that far from Cannes, which you've probably heard of."

"Uh, yep, Becky, I've definitely heard of Cannes," I answered.

Intrigued, I walked to Ms. Bouvier's desk to retrieve the letter. Signed by Daniel Mansanti, the mayor of Theoule-sur-Mer, the letter referenced the "liberation of the town" by American soldiers of the 141st Infantry Regiment on August 15th, 1944. During my tour as US defense attaché, I received several invitations to speak, not all of which I was able to accommodate, but this one was very interesting. My first inclination, before responding to Mayor Mansanti, was to do a little homework.

What happened on the French Riviera in World War II? I pondered. I had vaguely recalled that some US and allied military operations had been conducted there during the war, but I was not on firm ground about specific dates or actions, certainly not as much as I was for the more well-known—indeed, *far more* well-known—D-Day operations. As it turned out, the Provence Landings were no small affair. Originally intended to coincide with Normandy's D-Day but delayed due to the lack of landing craft, they involved some 300,000 allied troops over several days, half of whom were French, but many of whom hailed from French African nations. However, in spite of the magnitude of that combined allied military operation, many historians would refer to the Provence Landings as the "Forgotten D-Day." The Provence Landings were, nonetheless, undeniably critical to the war effort. Code-named Operation Dragoon, the southern France landings occurred some seventy days after the Operation Overlord landings on D-Day.

Winston Churchill initially resisted the Provence (including the French Riviera) Landings, preferring to concentrate all Allied forces in northern France. However, the Americans strongly preferred adding a second front to the European war effort as the southern arm of a strategic pincer movement against the German forces. It was the American concept that prevailed. The French also strongly backed Operation Dragoon, wanting to liberate the major southern cities of Marseille and Toulon with predominantly French troops.

With a broad operational concept similar to Normandy, the plan was to employ American and British airborne forces to disrupt the German defenses from behind. These forces jumped in the night of August 14, 1944, and were involved in heavy fighting, although some were lost at sea on what was a very foggy evening. The major amphibious assault occurred on a beautiful French Riviera morning of August 15, 1944, and involved the 3rd, 36th and 45th US Infantry Divisions. In all, the combined initial Allied landing force was estimated to be roughly 150,000. While exact figures are hard to determine, it was estimated that roughly 1,300 soldiers died in the first two days of the invasion.

On August 16, 1944, soldiers of the US 141st Infantry Regiment, 36th Infantry Division, who had already fought a tough campaign in Italy, liberated the town of Theoule-sur-Mer at the cost of nine soldiers. Theoule-sur-Mer is believed to have been the first town of the French Maritime Alps to have been liberated by the allied forces of the Provence Landings.

Overall, the strategic success of the Provence Landings cannot be disputed. On August 17, 1944, Adolf Hitler ordered a withdrawal of German forces back to the Vosges Mountains, where heavier fighting would later take place.

After knowing a bit more of the history of Theoule-sur-Mer and the Provence Landings, I gladly accepted Mayor Daniel Mansanti's invitation to participate in the town's sixtieth anniversary of its liberation by American soldiers.

Given the relatively long distance from Paris to Theoule-sur-Mer, roughly an eight- to nine-hour drive, I decided to fly. I also decided that I would do all the events without an embassy vehicle and driver, which were typically afforded to me for such occasions. This would not only save the US government money, it would also not disrupt the well-deserved vacation period of my driver, Thierry Fleuet, particularly during this most sacrosanct of French vacation periods. All of the expenses of the trip, including lodging and dining, were covered by my hosts, the city of Theoule-sur-Mer. Susan was also invited by the city to accompany me on this trip.

Theoule-sur-Mer is an idyllic village on the French Riviera, located roughly seven miles, or about eleven kilometers, west of Cannes, its more internationally known and much larger neighbor to the east. Dating back to the fifth century, the town is also part of the French Maritime Alps, which dominate this part of France's Mediterranean coastline. It is, as one might surmise, a lovely spot for a summer vacation.

While historians often refer to the Provence Landings of August 15, 1944, as the "Forgotten D-Day," nothing could be farther from the truth for the citizens of Theoule-sur-Mer. On or about August 16 of each and every year, they remember the nine American soldiers of the 141st Infantry Regiment, 36th Infantry Division (Texas National Guard) who sacrificed their lives in liberating the town. In addition to commemorating the soldiers of the 141st Infantry Regiment, the town also celebrates its liberation in partnership with ships of the United States and French navies, both of which participated in the Provence Landings of 1944. This sixtieth anniversary of the town's liberation, however, was to be a major affair. It was also one that Susan and I were very honored to be a part of.

Arriving on August 13, after checking into our accommodations at the Miramar Hotel, our first order of business was to meet with Mayor Daniel Mansanti at the *l'hôtel de ville,* which is not an actual hotel. *"L'hôtel de ville"* is the name given to city halls across France. Our initial meeting, all done in the French language, as it would be during our three full days there, was brief but very cordial.

"Good afternoon, Mr. Mayor, it is an honor and pleasure to meet you," I began. "You have a beautiful town here. I want to thank you for your very kind invitation to participate in your ceremonies."

"Colonel Steinke, we thank *you* and Mrs. Steinke for your willingness to travel down from Paris to be with us," he said.

"It is our honor to do so," I said.

After presenting him with a small memento from the US Embassy, I asked about confirmation for the next day's events.

"We will begin with a small welcome reception here in City Hall," he said. "It will include a couple of US and French naval officers, and a few members of the city council. After that, we will invite you to visit our public display just across the street from the city hall, which we have put together to mark this occasion."

"Mr. Mansanti, I am very much looking forward to the occasion," I said.

Before departing City Hall, I confirmed with a member of the mayor's staff that the short-sleeved, US Army "Class B" uniform would work best for the upcoming day's less formal events. Arriving mid-morning the next day, I was happy to see that the eleven naval officers, eight from France and three from the United States, including the commanders of the USS *Ramage* (DDG 61), an Arleigh Burke-class guided missile destroyer, and the French ship *Le Muse*, were wearing the same uniform, their short-sleeved all-whites uniforms.

The cordial welcome reception lasted about forty-five minutes and included gift exchanges with Mayor Mansanti. I felt truly welcomed by the mayor and his staff, as did Susan. While a couple of other spouses would later arrive, the U.S and French naval officers present on this first day did not have their spouses with them, so Susan was the only spouse there for the occasion.

Upon the conclusion of the reception, Mayor Mansanti invited us to visit the Information Center, which had been specifically established to mark the liberation sixtieth anniversary ceremonies. After a while, a handful of us, including Susan, wandered over to visit the "Salle d'Exposition," a large room full of newspaper clippings of the Provence Landings, of the liberation of the Theoule-sur-Mer, of books, maps, posters, and other periodicals of the era. As I stood there reading a bit of history about the Provence Landings and Theoule-sur-Mer, one of the exposition's organizers introduced me to an elderly, tan, silver-haired gentleman of medium height, wearing an open-collared shirt and sporty eyeglasses.

"Colonel Steinke, this is Pierre Cardin," she said.

"Mr. Cardin, I am pleased to meet you," I said in French.

"Likewise, Colonel," he replied.

As I began with some small talk—"This is quite the interesting exposition, isn't it?"—my mind was racing.

"Indeed it is," he responded.

The only *Pierre Cardin* I had ever heard of was a French—no, an *international*—fashion *icon*, a fashion mogul, an inventor, a leader, an entrepreneur who helped define the word *fashion* in the second half of the twentieth century, a man who was the fashion designer for heads of state, movie stars, and the Beatles, and who had won virtually every French and international award imaginable in his field. Oh, yes, and he was also a member of the French Academy of Fine Arts (founded in 1648) and the recipient of the French Legion of Honor (rank of commander). He also owned this place called *Maxim's* in Paris, which had its own success story. *Is this gentleman I am speaking with* that *Pierre Cardin?* I asked myself.

"And, sir, what brings you to this exposition?" I asked.

"I live nearby," he said.

"Oh, here in Theoule-sur-Mer?" I asked.

"Not right in the town," he responded. "But just up on the side of a mountain, not far from here."

I called Susan over to introduce her. Fortunately, her French had gotten quite good despite its slight Spanish accent, and she could easily hold her own in conversation.

As the three of us chatted a bit, Mr. Cardin revealed a little more of why this event meant something to him, beyond just his status as Theoule-sur-Mer's most famous resident.

"Colonel Steinke, I was a young man when Paris was liberated in August of 1944," he said. "I was very thankful, and I will *never* forget it."

I rarely questioned why I chose, as an American, the profession of arms as my calling for most of my adult life. However, there were a few brief moments when I wondered if perhaps another public service path—such as coaching, diplomacy, or education—was the better path not taken. I think most human beings are prone to similar thoughts upon occasion. At hearing those words about the liberation of Paris, by one of the world's most accomplished artists and entrepreneurs, those thoughts went in the dust bin of my mind.

Later that afternoon, after my visit, I received a call from the US Embassy.

"Colonel Steinke, this is Becky Bouvier," said the caller. "I just got word that you are going to get a police escort from Theoule-sur-Mer to the vicinity of Toulon, where the aircraft carrier *Charles-de*

Gaulle is located."

"A police escort? Really? I was going to drive myself," I replied.

"Well, I was given this number for you to call," said Ms. Bouvier. "You should be able to get more details from them."

After Ms. Bouvier read the phone number, I said, "Thank you, Becky. I will follow up."

Immediately after hanging up, I called the number Becky had provided. On the other end was a French gendarmes officer. Upon learning I was driving myself, he still insisted I be given a police escort from my hotel in Theoule-sur-Mer to the harbor of Toulon, where I would take a boat to the French aircraft carrier *Charles-de-Gaulle*, site of the major ceremony for the Sixtieth Anniversary of the Provence Landings. The event would include French President Jacques Chirac, as well as some African heads of state and the French military chiefs of staff.

Of course, I did not turn the gendarmes officer down, agreeing to be ready the following morning at my hotel. Meanwhile, I picked up my rental car for the next day's trip to Toulon.

The next morning, at the appointed hour, I met two motorcycle-mounted gendarmes in the hotel parking lot. They were apparently expecting me to be with a driver and embassy car. Instead, I told them I was driving a 307 Peugeot, a four-cylinder with manual clutch hatchback I was renting. After their initial surprise, they both chuckled mightily.

"Okay, Colonel, no problem. Just follow the lead motorcycle at all times," said the gendarmes sergeant.

"I certainly will," I said.

Fortunately, I had a lot of experience driving manual transmission cars, as I had owned a series of them over the years. I had also been to a defensive driving course or two and had driven successfully in places like Palermo and Naples, Italy. If you can drive in Naples, where distances between cars are often measured in millimeters, you can drive anywhere!

As we made our way through Theoule-sur-Mer's twisting roads and steep inclines and onto the highway, I couldn't believe that I was I *legally* driving like a banshee, ripping through the gears and high rpms Jackie Stewart-style (or so I liked to think) to keep up with the agile, quickly accelerating and motorcycle-mounted gendarmes, who I hoped were having as much fun as I was. A trip that should have taken about an hour and fifteen minutes took more like forty-five.

As I bid the two gendarmes officers farewell in Toulon, I had no idea why I had received that escort, or who insisted that it be provided. It was one of those serendipitous moments as a military attaché that I did not question, but certainly appreciated.

Arriving at the *Charles De Gaulle* aircraft carrier by a small boat that transported about thirty-five passengers at a time, I was impressed with the *De Gaulle's* enormous size. While I had seen aircraft carriers from the US Navy pier in Norfolk, Virginia, standing on this behemoth's main deck provided a completely different perspective. I soon realized the dark surface on the deck also absorbed heat. Along with the smell of hydraulics, this fact made it not the most comfortable place to be.

On board, there were about 150 guests or so, including French President Jacques Chirac, some heads of state or their representatives from former French colonies in Africa, as well as the French Armed Forces service chiefs. Surveying the crowd, I realized I was the only American soldier, at least in military uniform, on the carrier. In President Chirac's speech, he acknowledged the French allies who participated in the Provence Landings, including the United States and a half dozen or so African colonies that contributed troops to the landings and fighting that followed. I was honored to have represented the US Armed Forces at this event.

After a non-eventful return to the Miramar Hotel in Theoule-sur-Mer, I realized that Susan had a great day, as well.

"Well, guess where I spent my day," said Susan.

"Shopping in Cannes?" I asked.

"Ha-ha—no. I was the personal guest of Pierre Cardin," Susan said. "His home is absolutely amazing."

"Personal *guest*?" I asked.

"Yes . . . along with four other women," Susan said. "He was very gracious. We enjoyed some champagne and appetizers on the balcony of his home, with a magnificent view of the sea. The home was so cool, constructed without any right angles. We also had a very nice lady, who lived on a nearby boat, give us the grand tour of the place. She said that some folks refer to it as 'the bubble house.' I have never seen anything like it in the world."

The next day, August 16, 2004, began with a crystal-clear, bluebell sky. This day would include a few events in commemoration of the August 16, 1944 liberation of towns across France's Mediterranean coastline. The town of Theoule-sur-Mer, however, would celebrate in grand but very respectful style, all of which I was honored to be a part of with Mayor Mansanti, a few people of the city council, and Susan.

It included boat trips out to the USS *Ramage* and the French ship *Le Muse*, including the ceremonial dropping of flowers into the sea, to commemorate the fallen; a procession through the town with local leaders and a local French member of parliament, Mr. Christian Estrosi; speeches delivered by a local British Consular officer, a local French politician, and me, in the town square; the unveiling of a marble plaque in the town square, in honor of the soldiers of the US 141st Infantry Regiment; the laying of a wreath at a World War II monument just outside of town and farther up the mountainside; and one of the coolest beach parties I'd ever attended, complete with a Glen Miller-style band and dancing on the beach, with U.S and French naval officers and sailors in attendance; many local townspeople in attendance; and the man who I surmise provided some financial support for it all, Mr. Pierre Cardin.

Just as he had been on the first day I met him, Cardin showed himself to be exceptionally gracious, patient, and, as I got to converse with him longer, funny. He spent a great deal of time mingling with the guests and signing autographs, many of which were sought by officers of the USS *Ramage*. A man in his early eighties, he was full of energy and life.

As the evening and my official time in Theoule-sur-Mer concluded, I remembered the words Cardin had spoken to me on our first encounter, in reference to the August 1944 liberation of Paris:

"I was very thankful, and I will never forget it."

Nor will I ever forget the heartfelt remembrances of American sacrifice and the wonderful hospitality of Mayor Daniel Mansanti, Mr. Pierre Cardin, and the people of Theoule-sur-Mer.

CHAPTER 34

PARIS
VIEWS BUSH
REELECTION

AS THE SUMMER OF 2004 TRANSITIONED to the cooler late summer and early fall days in Paris, the US presidential campaign began to heat up. After several years overseas, my experience had generally been that European citizens were every bit as interested in US presidential elections as US citizens. Local media—print, television, radio, and online—are abuzz with pundits and opinions, and the US presidential race is the hot topic in coffee shops and at dinner parties. In France, in 2004, there was an added degree of interest sparked by the Democratic challenger, Senator John Kerry (D- MA).

The senator from Massachusetts had a French background. This made him the darling of many French citizens and an excellent foil to the "Texas cowboy," President George W. Bush, who had "needlessly started the war in Iraq" (or so I often heard). Given that eighty percent of the France's adult population (probably closer to ninety percent in more liberal Paris) was against the Iraq War, this came as no surprise. However, whenever French government officials or new acquaintances asked me where in the US I was from, I would always tell them, "I was born in El Paso, Texas, and I'm darn proud of it." After pausing to observe some folks' blank expressions and still others practically recoil at the word "Texas," I would then add, "But I was mostly raised in Michigan." It got to be a lot of fun to observe, at least in some cases, their predictable expression and demeanor changes at the mere mention of those two US states.

John Kerry had spent many summers at his maternal grandparents' home in Saint-Briac-sur-Mer, a village in the northwestern coastal region of Brittany. He spoke fluent French, having learned it at a Swiss boarding school and no doubt practicing it in France. One of his first cousins was Brice Lalonde, a former French green party leader and an environment minister in the early 1990s.

Accordingly, in France John Kerry had cache. He gave the anti-Bush crowd the hope of an internationalist who understood the world beyond America's coastlines, or so many French people thought. When John Kerry stayed in the posh Hotel Crillon, located adjacent to the US Embassy, it was one of the few times I saw the American flag fly over the hotel (the other time being Lance Armstrong's since-denounced victories of the Tour-de-France). Kerry's stay at the Crillon created almost as much buzz as Jenifer Lopez's stay there during the Paris debut of one of her movies, *Maid in Manhattan.*

A few weeks before election day, the Hotel Crillon made a special offer and announcement. It invited guests, many who were in the international press corps or senior local diplomats, to its large dining room for the viewing of the US Presidential election results on a large, cinema-sized TV screen. It would be like a Super Bowl viewing in a large American sports bar. Except this was about politics—*US presidential politics.*

As Tuesday, November 2, 2004 approached, there was a French buzz of hope that Senator John Kerry, with his French DNA, might actually have a shot at becoming the next President of the United States. On the early afternoon of November 2, I ventured over to the Hotel Crillon to see how the viewing was going. It was still rather quiet, with just a few people in attendance. It was still morning in America, so the only ongoing television discussions, mostly on CNN, involved pundits discussing recent straw polls and different electoral college scenarios, often involving key states like Florida and Ohio.

In the late evening of November 2, I headed back over to the Crillon. When I later departed, after midnight, the place was electrified, with Kerry leading slightly in the electoral college vote tally. By 2:00 a.m. in France and 8:00 p.m. on the US East Coast, Kerry was leading with seventy-seven electoral votes against George W. Bush's sixty-six. Much of France fell asleep late that night thinking John Kerry would be the next President of the United States.

As I awoke that morning of November 3 at 6:00 a.m., the US Presidential election had become a real horse race, with Bush leading by a nose and less than ten votes separating the two candidates, out of about 400 electoral votes counted by that point. I decided to head for the Hotel Crillon for the grand finale.

Taking the Paris metro to Place de la Concorde, I emerged from the metro's underground tunnel right in front of the Hotel Crillon. As I walked past the doorman, whom I'd seen almost daily on my way to and from the embassy, I saw that he had a gloomy look on his face. *He's probably just tired and about to leave his shift,* I thought.

Moving through the Hotel Crillon's revolving glass and brass door, I headed for the reviewing room with the big cinema-sized movie screen. As I walked in at around 7:15 a.m. it felt more like a presidential *library* than a presidential election viewing room. All I could hear, besides the occasional clinking of the china and silverware from the morning coffee and croissants being consumed, was a few muffled conversations here and there.

As I looked up to the movie screen, as far as this mostly sullen crowd was concerned, it seemed to say it all:

Electoral Vote Count: Bush—269; Kerry—207; Undecided—62.

During the roughly hour and fifteen minutes it took me to wake up and travel to the Hotel Crillon, the US states of Montana, Colorado,

Florida, Ohio, and Alaska had all been called for President Bush. The critical states of Florida and Ohio had provided 47 electoral votes for Bush. At this point, even if Kerry swept all remaining states, the best any Kerry supporter could hope for was a tie (with the deciding vote to be cast in the House of Representatives). All Bush would need would be one vote to get to the magic number of 270. By 11:30 a.m. Paris time, Kerry would somewhat close the gap, making it Bush 269 and Kerry 238. However, by late afternoon in Paris, it was "case closed," with Nevada's five electoral votes sealing the second presidential term for George W. Bush.

With his victory, a new presidential representative, Ambassador Craig Stapleton, would arrive in the middle of 2005 to take the helm of the US Embassy Paris country team.

CHAPTER 35

DIVINE INTERVENTION

"HEY, RICK, I'D LIKE TO bring Kelly to Paris for her big birthday," said the caller on the line. "Would it be okay if we visited you guys?"

"Mike, not only would it be okay to visit, Susan and I insist you stay with us!" I said. "When would you like to come over?"

"In early June, if that will work for you," he said.

"That will be perfect, Mike," I replied. "We might be a little busy then with Normandy events, but we look forward to it!"

As I hung up the phone, I was thrilled. As a friend, I had known Mike Fortino longer than anybody on the planet. We had met as eleven-year-old kids in Big Rapids, Michigan in 1967, a year after my father, Sergeant First Class Harvey F. Steinke, had retired from the Army. Mike and I would play as kids often did back then, joining together at some field—almost any field—for a game of baseball, and later for basketball in front of his well-worn garage, or riding our bikes somewhere.

After the Detroit Tigers beat the St. Louis Cardinals in the 1968 World Series, we played Wiffle ball, calling out the names of the Detroit Tigers—Kaline, McAuliffe, Freehan, Horton, Stanley, Cash, McLain, Lolich, Wert, Brown, Northrup, and Mathews, occasionally giving a nod to the Cardinals with an honorable mention to their great pitcher, Bob Gibson.

On a Saturday on or right after the opening day of trout season in April, Mike, and I would get up at about 4:30 a.m. and leave his house in Big Rapids and head for nearby Mitchell Creek. We would be fishing at first light, and if we caught a brook trout or two, it was a great day. (Today, unfortunately, it would be unheard of to let eleven- and twelve-year-old kids out of the house at that hour to go fishing. But in small-town Midwest America, circa the 1960s and 1970s, I'm sure this was a scene repeated many times over.) If you've ever seen the movie *Stand By Me* (1986), that was Mike and me. We were pretty much on our own as long as we were home by dark.

We had thick skins too. Although my paternal grandmother, nee Virginia Brockway, could trace her English roots to the "first pioneer child" born in Mecosta County, Michigan, on February 12, 1853, near the very same Mitchell Creek Mike and I would fish, and even though I was born in Texas, because of my obviously German last name and because my family had arrived in Big Rapids from Germany just after my father had completed a two-year Army tour, I was called "Kraut." And I was totally okay with it. It was who I was. Besides, it was never said by a friend—or anybody else, for that matter—with an impugning tone. It was a simple nickname.

My heritage was indeed mainly German, with some English and Alsatian roots (my German mother's maiden name was Schlumberger, pronounced differently in French and German) as well. Mike, on the other hand, had a Sicilian father and Lebanese mother. He was called "Wop." While the "without papers" acronym was a misnomer (Mike was born in the US, as was his father), it was in reference to Mike's Italian background. Mike was okay with that "Wop" moniker too.

However, even at twelve or thirteen years old, Mike and I *knew* one thing, *by God*: we were *Americans*. There was never a doubt about that or about not "fitting in."

Neither Mike Fortino nor I had ever had a prejudiced bone in our bodies (and it confounds and pains me to see how, as of this writing, racial prejudice has made a comeback in America). We also knew instinctively there were limits to these adolescent labels, which faded the farther we got into high school. We knew, for example, that the N-word was highly offensive. It was a word that never crossed our lips nor those of the other overwhelmingly white kids, and later teenagers, we hung out with.

Both of our fathers had served for a time in the Army. My dad had dropped out of high school in 1944 and enlisted in the Army, arriving in Germany in 1945, not long after the war's end. He eventually would serve from 1948-1954 in one unit: the 54th Engineer Combat Battalion (today it would be "Combat Engineer"). Mike's father, Jim, on the other hand, had served in World War II in Europe. Both of our dads were members of the local Big Rapids American Legion, getting together to play poker almost weekly. (Occasionally, they would have a beer too many, much to the irritation of our mothers.) On most Sundays, Mike's family would head to St. Mary's Catholic Church, and the Steinkes would attend St. Peter's Lutheran Church, where my grandfather and grandmother, Alfred and Virginia Steinke, were plank holders.

As I was lying on Mike's living room floor one Sunday afternoon, watching a late season Detroit Lions game, a TV advertisement for the future release of the movie *Patton* came on. Mike's father Jim suddenly blurted out, "That son-of-a-bitch, George Patton! His guts . . . and our blood!"

Jim was referring to Lieutenant General George S. Patton's nickname, "ole Blood and Guts," given to him by US soldiers who both revered and feared him. It was as if he had a visceral, reflexive reaction to the name "Patton," a name which also struck fear in many a heart of the German Wehrmacht formations which faced his Third Army divisions in combat.

No doubt a flood of memories had returned with Jim's viewing of the *Patton* movie ad. For some reason I remembered that incident some thirty-plus years after the fact, when Mike said he was coming to France, wondering if he might be able to learn something about his dad's service. Mike's dad had passed away in the 1980s, and in classic World War II veteran fashion, had never talked to Mike about his service in World War II.

"Mike, do you have any military papers from your dad's discharge from the Army?" I asked him. "It will probably be a Form DD 214 or something like that, which summarizes his military service on a single page. If you can find that, we might be able to learn something about his service in Europe."

"I think I do have something like that around the house," he said. "When I find it, I'll make a copy and send it over."

About two weeks later, via snail mail, I received an envelope from Grayling, Michigan. In the envelope was a copy of what was obviously a well-worn original of James Fortino's service record. Fortunately, it was still legible.

The one-page record noted that Jim Fortino had landed on Omaha Beach with his field artillery battalion, the 37th Field Artillery (105 mm) of the US 2nd Infantry Division on D-Day + 1, June 7, 1944. By that time, the capture of "bloody Omaha" beach, so realistically portrayed in the movie *Saving Private Ryan*, was complete. However, the 2nd Division would soon find itself in combat and the hellish struggle to break out of the Normandy area that would be aggressively contained by the German Wehrmacht for over eight weeks.

From shortly after joining the fight in the Normandy region, the 2nd US Infantry Division would be involved in 303 days of combat, with 2,999 men killed and 10,924 wounded. Jim Fortino fought from St. Laurent-sur-Mer, France, across the entire country and again across all of Germany, from west to east. His war came to an end on V-E Day, May 8, 1945, in a town called Pilsen, in what is now the Czech Republic. (Pilsen is more famously known to beer drinkers around the world as the place that gave its name to Pilsner beer.) After I reviewed Jim Fortino's service record, I made a mental note of it, but did not give it a second thought.

In the meantime, in terms of scale, the sixty-first anniversary of D-Day would be a far lesser event than the previous year's sixtieth. I was asked by the curators of the Omaha Beach Museum if I might address a group of D-Day veterans there from the 75th Rangers as well as the 1st and 29th Infantry Divisions, on the 5th of June.

"It will be my honor and privilege," I responded.

As Mike and Kelly had arrived in Paris a few days prior to the Omaha Beach Museum event, we decided to travel up to Omaha Beach together, but not before we shared an incredible dinner in the Eiffel Tower with Susan. She was not, however, able to make this trip up to Normandy with us, as the girls were still in school.

Once in the Normandy area, I took Mike and Kelly to the Normandy American Cemetery at Colleville-sur-Mer and then to the event at the Omaha Beach Museum. In my speech, humbly delivered to about thirty heroes of D-Day, I wove Jim Fortino's landing at Omaha Beach and subsequent fighting in Europe into the words. Mike got the whole thing on tape. I believe he was quite touched by the gesture.

After the Omaha Beach Museum event, we contemplated whether to drive back to Paris right away, or get a bite to eat first. We were really quite undecided, but then I remembered Le Sapiniere restaurant on Omaha Beach, the place where I had gone at least a half dozen times with the White House advance team just a year previously. I figured we could take a drive down to the beach and decide along the way.

Engaged in spirited conversation, we decided to kill a few minutes before going for some seafood at Le Sapiniere. As I drove and we chatted, I did something I had *never* done during any previous trips to Omaha Beach proper: I drove *past* Le Sapiniere.

Perhaps a quarter or half mile or so down the beach past Le Sapiniere, as I was just about to look for a place to turn around, I spied what looked to be a monument back in the trees, perhaps thirty to forty yards out. I suggested we get out of the car and have a look, as we continued to talk and enjoy each other's company. As the three of us got out of the car, my gait picked up, and I instinctively stepped out ahead to discover this curious monument that I had not been aware existed.

And then I saw it: on the black marble monument, facing my direction, was the unmistakable relief of *the Indianhead centered on a star*. It was the symbol of the US 2nd Infantry Division, the "Indianhead division," the same one with which Jim Fortino had landed on Omaha Beach, and with which he had fought for over 300 days. It was a division that became part of Lieutenant General George S. Patton's Third Army. I had had no idea the monument was on the beach until that moment.

My mind flashed back to Jim Fortino, lying on his couch in late 1969, blurting out, "That son-of-a-bitch, George Patton!" Now, it all came together, it all made sense. With massive goosebumps, I felt God's Spirit tingle my soul. I thought of Jim Fortino and Harvey Steinke smiling down upon us from heaven.

All the while, as we got closer to the monument and I explained out loud what I was seeing, Mike had his video camera running. With tears filling his eyes, he was "talking" to his older brother Buzz (or Buzzy) Fortino, all the while explaining to Buzz the very special discovery he was now filming.

Obviously, we had been indecisive about going back to Paris for a *reason*. We had been indecisive about having dinner for a *reason*. And I drove past Le Sapiniere for the *first time* after almost three years in France, and perhaps a dozen or so previous trips to Omaha Beach, for a *reason*.

Back in Paris the next evening, I took Mike down to the deep, dark, 120-year-old basement storage room that doubled as my wine cellar. I pulled out four bottles of the best wine I had, saved for a special occasion. The wines included St. Julian and Pomerol from the Bordeaux region, Barolo from the Italian Piedmont region, and Amarone from the Italian Veneto region. Susan made French *confit de canard*, or "crispy duck" as Mike liked to call it.

That evening, Susan, Kelly, Mike, and I shared some special hours over the kind of meal that only comes around every so often in a lifetime.

CHAPTER 36

NEW EMBASSY LEADERSHIP

"BRANDY, THIS IS RICK," I said on the phone to the ambassador's executive assistant, Brandy Lowe. "Is the rumor true? Is Ambassador Leach moving on this summer?"

"Yes, it is Rick," she replied. "Howard will be moving on."

"Do you know about when that will be?" I asked.

"Sometime early in the summer, I suspect," she said. "Perhaps June, or maybe earlier."

"And do you know who will replace him?" I asked.

"Yes, I do. At least, I know who is *intended* to replace him," she said. "It's Ambassador Craig Stapleton, who currently serves as US Ambassador to the Czech Republic."

"Well, I'm sorry Ambassador Leach is leaving," I said. "He's been great to work for."

"He's not going far, Rick," she said. "He bought a place in Paris, so he'll be around for quite some time."

"Good for him," I said. "And Brandy, thanks for the intel."

"Anytime, Rick."

The news from Brandy was a bit surprising. Leach had been, at least in my opinion, quite effective during some of the more troubled years in the long arch of the US-France relationship, dating back to America's Revolutionary War. My teammates in the DAO all agreed we wanted to present the ambassador a memento upon his departure, which we did, providing him with a framed print of the Ecole Militaire.

Just who was this Craig Stapleton Brandy had mentioned? Was he a political appointee, or a career foreign service officer? More importantly, what would his leadership style be like? Was he aloof or engaging? What did he think about the value of his defense attaché and defense attaché team in Prague? What would my fourth and final year of military attaché service be like with Craig Stapleton in charge?

As I began to do some homework, querying a few contacts in US Embassy Prague as well as Paris, I was hearing good things about his leadership style. That was encouraging. But I decided to dig a little deeper.

A *cum laude* graduate of Harvard University, Craig Stapleton also had an MBA from Harvard. A very successful businessman, he had served as President of Marsh and McLennan Real Estate Advisors of New York from 1982 until 2000, in addition to serving on the boards of directors for several other companies. From 1989 to 1998 he also co-owned the Texas Rangers baseball team with George W. Bush. His relationship with the Bush family went beyond the professional, as his wife, Dorothy Walker Stapleton, was a first cousin of President George Herbert Walker Bush.

Not long after he took over US Embassy Paris, he and his deputy chief of mission, Karl Hoffman, went about making some changes. In addition to the larger country team meeting, which was held once a week with over twenty-five embassy officials and agency representatives in attendance, he instituted a smaller US embassy senior leader meeting, with eight to ten department or agency senior leaders of the embassy, of which I was honored to be a part. This meeting was held in his office, where the fireplace mantle now had a picture of him, President George W. Bush, and Florida governor Jeb Bush, looking pretty relaxed at a Texas Rangers baseball game. The weekly meeting was very collegial and inclusive, and also very effective for keeping good situational awareness with respect to US-France issues, France-Europe issues, and internal embassy agenda items.

While the US "punish France" policy had waned significantly during the last year of Leach's tenure, it was clear with Stapleton's arrival that that era was about to be officially and completely over. Within a few weeks Stapleton invited the French chief of defense, General Henri Bentégeat, to the United States to meet with the leaders of US Central Command; US Special Operations Command; and US Joint Forces Command, as well as the chairman of the Joint Chiefs of Staff, General Richard Myers. I accompanied General Bentégeat on that trip.

A trip highlight was attending a dinner hosted in honor of Bentégeat by General Richard Myers at Fort Myer, Virginia. The dinner included some people I knew, including Susan Eisenhower, Brigadier General (Ret.) John and Barbara Eisenhower's daughter and President Dwight D. "Ike" and Mamie Eisenhower's granddaughter. Susan and I had met at Harvard during the 1998–1999 school year. An expert on US-Russia relations and Russian political affairs, among other things, she had served as a senior fellow at Harvard's John F. Kennedy School of Government.

My dinner tablemates included Vice-Admiral Mike Mullens, who would later become chairman of the Joint Chiefs of Staff; and former Army lieutenant and television journalist Sam Donaldson. Donaldson was a riot to sit next to. While I often thought he was a bit aggressive as a White House correspondent (I could still hear him yelling, "Mr. President! Mr. President!" at President Ronald Reagan), he was a wonderful and quite funny conversationalist.

The Bentégeat trip would be General Myers's last major engagement with a foreign chief of defense: he would retire three weeks later. As it concluded he awarded Bentégeat with the US Legion of Merit. From my humble perspective, this act put a period on the last sentence of the "punish France" saga.

Once back in Paris, I observed that Stapleton was also heavily engaged in bringing in prominent leaders for their experience and knowledge of international relations and relevant themes. They included President George Herbert Walker Bush, Dr. Henry Kissinger, and select justices of the Supreme Court. As embassy leaders, many of us were afforded access to these highly successful and prominent practitioners of diplomacy, international relations, and law.

With each passing week, I became very impressed with not only Stapleton's inclusive management style, approachability, and personal engagement, but also his tireless work ethic. In the Pentagon, senior Army officers have a reputation for driving themselves incessantly, often working fourteen-hour days (often translating into a 5:00 a.m. arrival and 7:00 p.m. departure, with some days being even longer). Craig Stapleton was not quite at that level of intense and sustained activity. But he worked hard, very hard.

His security detail officers informed me he would often leave work at 5:30 p.m., play a round of squash, and then begin his often two-diplomatic-events-per-night routine, not getting home until 10:00 p.m. or later. He followed this routine for three to four nights each week.

His weekends were also often taken up with diplomatic events. One included a trip to the St. Cyr Military Academy, the French equivalent of West Point (and founded the same year, 1802). While accompanying him on this trip, he delivered a speech to St. Cyr cadets and faculty on the state of US military affairs around the globe. He answered most of the questions quite competently on his own, deferring to me only on questions of tactical or operational import. We made a good team, and I enjoyed the heck out of working with and for him.

I know sometimes both US Foreign Service officers and even foreign diplomats rail at the mainly US concept of politically appointed ambassadors, citing their lack of diplomatic experience, international naiveté, or worse. In my opinion, that absolutely could not be said about Craig Roberts Stapleton. I believe his 100-percent-committed and all-in service to the United States was an absolute bargain for the American taxpayer.

CHAPTER 37

CHINESE "RECEPTION"

APPROACHING THE NINETEENTH-CENTURY BUILDING where the Chinese Embassy was hosting a reception not far from the Arch of the Triumph, I was quite curious as to what this evening would bring. I was also very much looking forward to it. After being in Paris for over three years, I'd never before received an invitation from the Chinese Embassy. In fact, it was the first invitation any US DAO Paris team member had received in quite some time to an official Chinese event.

I knew my new Marine attaché, Lieutenant Colonel Ben Moody, would be there. While previously assigned to Marine Helicopter Squadron One (HMX-1), the unit that flies for the President of the United States, Ben had served as the operational test director for the V-22 Osprey. He and his wife, Lorie, herself a Marine reserve officer, had made a superb addition to the DAO Paris team.

As I climbed the steps, minus Susan for this event, to the reception's street-side entrance and entered through the main doors, I soon realized there was no receiving line. Looking ahead, I could see that most folks were standing in a buffet line. *Some real Chinese food ought to provide a good conversation starter tonight*, I thought.

As I surveyed the crowd and was about to join the buffet line, Moody stepped directly in front of me. Standing beside him was Major Chad Lemond, assistant Army attaché.

With his face just a few inches from mine, Ben said, "Sir, I need to let you know there is a guy with a big TV camera, followed around by another man and a woman. At first thinking I might be you, the man asked if the US defense attaché had arrived. I told him you weren't here, and that I was not sure if you were coming."

"Thanks much for the heads-up, Ben," I replied.

I then joined the buffet line, observing who else was at this event, and then eyeing some of the offerings. Within about three minutes, while reaching for a spring roll, I felt a tap on my shoulder. As I turned around, I could see the shoulder-mounted TV camera Moody had warned me about. Pointed right at my face, it was perhaps three feet away. Standing in front and just off to the side of the cameraman was a tall Chinese man, well over six feet, with a microphone in his hand. Standing beside him was a younger and shorter Chinese lady, perhaps in her late twenties, with a notepad and pen at the ready, looking eager, as if she was on her first assignment as a journalist. Within seconds, without any self-introduction or explanation, the man with the microphone held it close to my mouth, with the light of the TV camera shining on me.

"What you think of the Chinese *military threat*?" he asked.

I briefly hesitated before I replied.

"Chinese military threat?" I asked. "Are you *telling* me there is a Chinese military threat?" I replied, countering his question with another.

My Chinese questioner did not answer.

Another pause ensued, this one a bit longer.

"Because I don't see a Chinese military threat," I continued. "I believe we are cooperating in many areas, are we not? In fact, I know of a US Army major who is training in your country as we speak."

A former Army lieutenant of mine from the 1st Battalion, 27th

Field Artillery Regiment, who was now a major, had just written me an email briefly describing his travels in China as he was in training to become a US Army Foreign Area Officer.

Another pause followed, after which the TV camera light went off and my welcoming party just walked away. I don't remember hearing "thank you for your time" or "welcome to the Chinese embassy reception" or "enjoy a spring roll." They just walked away without another word.

As they did, I wondered what Chinese military propaganda or training film our sweet little interview might end up in. I did not have to wonder, however, if I would accept another invitation from the Chinese embassy in Paris. Skipping the spring rolls, I departed from the reception.

CHAPTER 38

DINNER WITH THE FRENCH ARMY CHIEF OF STAFF

AS I RETURNED HOME VIA the Paris metro on a cool evening in early May 2006, I was excited to give Susan some news about an invitation for an event to be held in late May. We had received well over 150 invitations to various events in the roughly forty-four months we'd been in Paris, but this one, as we were nearing the end of our tour, was special.

"Sweetie, guess who we will be having dinner with later this month?" I said.

"Oh, I don't know . . . Armand Assante, maybe?" she quipped, referring to the actor on whom she'd held a crush for quite some time. "Or Johnny Depp? Or maybe Laura Bush?" she asked.

"Uh, well . . . *no*," I answered. "It's the *Thorettes*," I said, adding for emphasis, "General and Mrs. Thorette."

"That is wonderful," said Susan. "Seriously, that is something very much to look forward to. They have both been very kind and gracious to us."

Indeed they had been. While we had also had the honor of

hosting both General and Mrs. Thorette for a dinner in our Paris apartment, we had been hosted at receptions at least five or six times in either their historic quarters in Les Invalides, or at other separate venues, such as at the nearby French Military Museum. We genuinely liked them as people.

For his part, General Thorette appreciated—and was perhaps even a bit charmed by—Susan's Spanish-accented French (which he commented on in their first encounter). Anne-Marie Thorette, although a fully employed anesthetist, somehow managed to appear at her husband's side for most events as a model of class and grace. From my perspective, it's odd how certain things come to mind when thinking of someone after many years. In Anne-Marie Thorette's case, I'll never forget what bothered her most about this world we live in. "Injustice," she said.

Professionally, General Bernard Thorette always treated me, an Army colonel, as an equal to the British and German defense attachés, not to mention other attachés, who were general officers. After a French military scandal erupted in the Ivory Coast, I found myself in General Thorette's office along with the German defense and army attaché, Brigadier General Harald Quiel, and the British army attaché, Brigadier General Tim Gregson, getting the inside story—beyond the distorted accounts and speculation in the media—directly from the top leader of the French Army.

On the evening of our dinner with General and Mrs. Thorette, as our embassy car approached Les Invalides, my mind wandered to the many events I had attended there, some with Susan and some without. Perhaps the most notable occurred in the Les Invalides courtyard some two years prior, when the French government bestowed Legion of Honor medals to 100 American veterans of D-Day. It was an event that conveyed that, in spite of the political disagreements that will occur in any political relationship spanning over 200 years, America's oldest ally always remembers the great sacrifices of its trans-Atlantic partner.

Ascending the steps to General and Anne-Marie Thorette's quarters, Susan and I did not know who else would be at the dinner. As we had upon other occasions, we met General and Mrs. Thorette at the door, exchanging the normal pleasantries, while presenting them with a framed etching of the *White House and North Patio* by the American artist, Don Connavaro. As we entered the hallway, which obscured the view from the rest of the magnificent apartment, we could hear a few voices. Turning the corner, we recognized three or four French officers and their spouses. This was a bit unexpected, because virtually every single official dinner or social event Susan and I had attended to that point with General and Mrs. Thorette was multinational, not binational as this one was shaping up to be.

As we were seated at the same table where I had previously dined with senior American military guests (such as General Burwell B. "BB" Bell, Commander, US Army Europe), General Thorette began:

"Rick and Susan, this dinner is for you. It has been a great pleasure for Anne-Marie and I to know both of you over the past three-plus years. You have been splendid representatives of America and the United States Army. Rick, it has been my honor to serve with you, and I would like to give you a small token of my appreciation," said General Thorette.

At this point, his aide-de-camp brought him an oval-shaped bottle with what looked to be a dark brown liquid inside. I could see from where I sat that the bottle had, in big and bold numbers, the year of my birth on it, but I could make out little else of the fine print.

"Colonel Steinke, I think you know we French like our brandy," he said. "But this one is quite special. It's Armagnac, and as the oldest brandy in France, it comes from the southwest, one of my favorite parts of the country. And I hope we got your birth year correct!" he said.

"You did indeed, sir," I responded. "I thank you, and I am humbled to receive this very special gift from you. It has been an honor and privilege to serve with you as well, and for Susan and me to get to know Anne-Marie over these preceding years."

On the bottle's label, which I could now read, it said (translated from French), "Specially selected and bottled for Colonel STEINKE on behalf of General of the Army, THORETTE." General Thorette signed the label, "*très amicalement.*"

Reflecting on the previous three-plus years, I was thinking how fortunate I was to have served with this French general and gentleman during my time as Defense and Army Attaché to France. Even though I had been one of the bearers of bad news on that day in May 2003, in which he was humiliated by the US Marine War College's last-minute "change of plans," General Bernard Thorette had never wavered in his professionalism and goodwill toward the United States Army or United States Marine Corps (or me, for that matter). In a couple of weeks, I would see him one more time at my farewell reception at the US Ambassador's residence. Thorette, chief of staff of the French Army and the officer who commanded the French marine regiment which protected the US's—and coalition's—left flank during Operation Desert Storm, would retire with distinction some two months later.

CHAPTER 39

SEEKING FLEM
STAPLETON

"RICK, AMBASSADOR STAPLETON WOULD LIKE to visit a local American cemetery for Memorial Day," said the ambassador's secretary. "Assuming you have no other commitments, he was wondering if you'd like to accompany him."

"I'd be delighted to," I said. "Do you know which one he'd like to visit?"

"Most likely Oise-Aisne," she said.

"Great, I'll put it on the calendar," I responded.

"Oh, by the way, he was also inquiring if you might be able to provide him some information on the Meuse-Argonne offensive," she said.

"Is he interested in anything particular?" I asked.

"Not really, just a summary of the battle, I think," she said.

As it was three weeks before Memorial Day 2006, and three and a half weeks before my retirement ceremony from the US Army, I was glad I had received no other commitments for this Memorial Day. Or perhaps I had, and Becky Bouvier declined them for me or rerouted them to another attaché in our office. I could think of nobody—other than my immediate family—with whom I would have rather commemorated Memorial Day with, particularly this last one as defense attaché, than Ambassador Craig Stapleton.

In the past ten months since his arrival at US Embassy Paris, Craig Stapleton had shown himself a completely dedicated representative of the President of the United States and American people in France. His support of my DAO team as well US-France military relations was almost unconditional, always making himself available for senior visiting US military personnel, or to speak with French military leaders and personnel, such as during our visit to the St. Cyr military academy.

Not long after the phone call from the ambassador's secretary, I began to research the World War I Meuse-Argonne offensive. In brief, I discovered—or rediscovered, after having first learned about it some thirty years prior—that it was one of the largest military offensives in history. Conducted from September 26 through November 11, 1918, its primary intent was to be so decisive for the Allies as to victoriously bring the war to its conclusion. This it successfully did, but at a great price, finally forcing the Germans to surrender at 11:11 a.m. on November 11, 1918.

Led first by General John J. "Black Jack" Pershing and later Lieutenant General Hunter Liggett, the Allied Expeditionary Force, with more than a million men under arms, had suffered 26,277 killed, 95,786 wounded, and well over 1,000 missing (including 954 names listed at the American Meuse Argonne Cemetery) during the great Meuse-Argonne offensive. Instead of being sent home, many fallen doughboys were interred in the dark soil of the French countryside, or their names were inscribed on US American Battle Monument Cemetery walls as "Missing."

As I met Ambassador Stapleton at the Residence before heading out to Oise-Aisne cemetery on May 29, 2006, it was a glorious, crisp, bluebell-sky morning. I thought his choice to visit Oise-Aisne cemetery on this Memorial Day was interesting, especially after he asked me to research the great Meuse-Argonne Offensive. Those American doughboys who fought in the Meuse-Argonne offensive of World War I were buried at the Meuse Argonne American cemetery, roughly ninety minutes by car east of the Oise-Aisne cemetery.

Interred at Oise-Aisne, on the other hand, were those who mainly fought in the Marne-Aisne campaign, which began with the decisive and desperate stand by the French, British, and American troops at the Marne River (Second Battle of the Marne), in defense of Paris. It was in this battle that the 3rd US Infantry Division earned its famous moniker, the "Rock of the Marne." After this backs-against-the-wall defense, perhaps one of their most precarious points in the war, the Allies successfully counterattacked. Most of the Americans buried at Oise-Aisne cemetery were from that battle.

After about a ninety-minute ride across the lovely verdant French landscape, part of it including the rolling hills of French Champagne country, we arrived at the high and pillared gates of the cemetery.

"This is quite some place, isn't it?" said Ambassador Stapleton, as we passed through the Oise-Aisne cemetery gates.

"It is, indeed, sir. It is, indeed," I replied as the ambassador's armored limousine moved slowly through the sea of white marble crosses and we approached the memorial at the end of the road. No matter how many times I visited an American Battle Monuments Commission cemetery, each time, it invoked a feeling of deep respect and gratitude.

Oise-Aisne was about 100 acres smaller than its Meuse-Argonne neighbor to the east. To us, driving slowly through it, it had more of an intimate feel than the larger Meuse-Argonne Cemetery.

As we stopped in the visitor's parking area, Ambassador Stapleton got out of the car, and I was right behind him. He was met by the cemetery's superintendent, Dave Bedford.

"Good morning, sir, welcome to Oise-Aisne cemetery," said Superintendent Bedford.

"Mr. Bedford, we are honored to be here," replied Stapleton.

After a quick self-introduction, the three of us walked to the memorial, adjacent to the chapel. The first thing that struck me from the outside was the rose-colored sandstone with white trim encompassing the memorial colonnade, containing relief sculptures of World War I. Although I had not seen all the ABMC cemeteries in France, I had seen most, and this was the first constructed with this beautiful rose sandstone. Centered inside the semi-arched and open-air colonnade was a white altar. Carved in the stone behind the altar was a doughboy (perhaps ten feet tall) standing at attention, holding the upper barrel of his vertical rifle with its stock on the ground.

As we entered the chapel doors, we beheld a black marble altar. Above and to the left of it, carved in rose sandstone, were many names.

"Engraved upon these Walls of the Missing are 241 names. Rosettes mark the names of those since recovered and identified," said the superintendent.

After about a minute of silence, Ambassador Stapleton responded:

"Last September, on 9/11, I visited the Meuse Argonne American Cemetery. This year, I wanted to visit this one, since my family has a connection with World War I."

As I looked at Stapleton's eyes, I could see they had welled up.

"Oh, and what was that?" I asked.

"We had a soldier from our family go missing in World War I," he said.

"What was the soldier's name?" asked Bedford.

"Flem Stapleton," said the ambassador. "He was from Paintsville, Kentucky."

I had no idea about Flem Stapleton. But I could still see the emotion, and pride, in the US Ambassador to France's eyes when he spoke the name.

As our tour continued, Bedford left the ambassador and me for about twenty minutes, as we walked among the crosses, pointing out various names and information of interest. Intermittently, we chatted casually with a couple and a family at the cemetery, none of whom would learn he was the US ambassador to France. Due to the significant time elapsed since the Great War, most American visitors, when coming to Europe for Memorial Day or other times, would visit the more recent World War II cemeteries. As a result, Oise-Aisne was lightly visited.

At one point, Stapleton asked, "Rick, why were there so many missing during World War I?"

"Two reasons, sir," I began. "Although back then there was something similar to what we know today as a dog tag, there wasn't a good system for—nor emphasis on—soldier accountability. World War II, on the other hand, saw the advent of graves registration units. These were units whose sole purpose in life—or in death, more accurately—was to account for fallen soldiers. The other reason, sadly, was the destructiveness of the weaponry back then, particularly the heavy artillery and mortars. Some of the shells were as big as Volkswagens."

After a while, Bedford came back.

"Sir, Flem Stapleton went missing on September 12th, 1918. It was during the Meuse-Argonne Offensive," he said. "He was an infantry private in the 9th Regiment, 2nd Infantry Division."

There it was *again*: the *2nd Infantry Division*.

It was the same US Army Division Mike Fortino's dad, Jim Fortino, had served in during World War II. How coincidental was it that out of all the US Army Divisions—well over 100—in both wars, that both Jim Fortino from Big Rapids, Michigan and Flem Stapleton from Paintsville, Kentucky would fight in the same division on European soil, some twenty-six years apart?

As it turned out, Kentucky provided over 84,000 men to serve in the US armed forces during World War I (not all of whom deployed to France). Of these, 2,418 died.

After departing the cemetery and sharing a French lunch

together, the ambassador and I returned to Paris. We had rendered our respects to Flem Stapleton and the brave "doughboys" of the Great War who paid the ultimate sacrifice for our—and Western Europe's—freedom, at least for another generation.

CHAPTER 40

RETIREMENT AND REFLECTIONS

AS WAS OFTEN THE CASE during the fourteen moves I had made in twenty-eight years of Army service, my last official duty week was quickly upon my family and me. I had decided to retire at twenty-eight years rather than the full (and mandatory) thirty for a US Army colonel because I wanted Erika (who was just about to graduate from the eighth grade) to have a complete four years at one high school, rather than moving her somewhere in the middle of that experience. Under almost any scenario, retirement at the thirty-year mark would have precluded her from completing four years at one school. I did mention to Susan my desire to serve for a final year in Afghanistan or Iraq, but that only brought a flood of tears, so I dropped the idea.

However, I couldn't get the thought out of my mind, or soul, as I would later volunteer as a Department of Defense (DoD) civilian, as part of the DoD Civilian Expeditionary Workforce, serving as the US Embassy Kabul's Senior Civilian Liaison to the Commander, ISAF Joint Command (IJC) in Kabul, Afghanistan. I was not leading soldiers in the field, but it was the best I could do. While I accompanied IJC's Commander, Lieutenant General David Rodriguez, we met with many military and civilian leaders in the field, while traveling to most every corner of that vast country. An experienced combat commander, "General Rod" knew it was a pain for subordinate field commanders whenever higher-level officials visited, so he always made the visits as low-profile but worthwhile as possible, speaking directly to as many leaders and soldiers as time and circumstances would allow.

A flurry of activity during our last official week in Paris included Erika graduating from the eighth grade at the American School of Paris and Maria from the second grade. The farewell before retiring and moving on to retirement from the US Army was a long one with several events. It was also supported by many people.

Ambassador Craig Stapleton graciously hosted a lunch with some of my international attaché colleagues and friends in the Residence. He also kindly held an evening farewell reception for Susan and me in the Residence. I was humbled by his complimentary remarks and touched by his presentation to me of a US Embassy memento. Swiss Lieutenant General Jacques Dousse, the Dean of the Paris Military Attachés, gave remarks, too, and he was as funny and witty as ever.

I was also humbled and overwhelmed by the attendees—more than 100—which included General Bentégeat and his wife, Chantal, who graciously befriended and hosted Susan on several occasions; Army Chief of Staff General Bernard Thorette; Major General Vincent Desportes, who would later command the French Ecole Militaire, and his wife, Anne; my old friend and French Colonel (Ret.) Charlie Deleris; and many other French and international officers and friends. They also included all of my then-serving and phenomenal Defense Attaché Office teammates. Among them were attache teammates who had arrived in the second half of my tour: Colonel Mike Guillot, Air Attache; and Major Ryan Pendleton, Assistant Air Attache; as well as Major Mike Vassalotti, who was serving as the liaison officer to the French Joint Staff.

Also present was the officer whom I admired and respected most in the United States Army at the time, Major General Ken Hunzeker,

Commanding General of the storied 1st US Infantry Division, the "Big Red One." His wife, Patty, was there, too, having traveled from Wurzburg, Germany for the event. I had served as Ken's battalion operations, plans, and training officer, and he had graciously agreed to preside at my retirement ceremony.

The next day, my retirement ceremony was held in the US Embassy. It was essentially a US event, so Ambassador Stapleton again gave heartfelt opening remarks. General Hunzeker did a wonderful job in leading the entire event. He had been prepared to include our daughters, Erika and Maria, in the ceremony, but Susan and I had decided to keep them in school for the day. We strongly believed in not taking them out of school unless absolutely necessary (they had near-perfect attendance records). However, I later realized that was a mistake. I should have had them there to be part of this very special and transitional event, which the US Army does as well as any service. It would have also perhaps helped Erika and Maria (less so, given her age) to better understand the major transition we were about to go through.

My mother, Erika, for whom our older daughter Erika was named, had flown in from Florida, and my only sibling, my brother Chris, also flew in from Texas. Their attendance also made the event very special.

During my retirement speech, when I mentioned Susan and the girls, I choked up, wondering if I'd be able to finish. At one point I mentioned the word "marathon," and Ken Hunzeker, seeing I was struggling with my emotions, called out, "pick up the pace!" That caused the audience—and fortunately, me—to laugh out loud, and I was then able to continue speaking.

A couple of days later, Ken, Patty, Susan, and I headed for the Bordeaux region, where we sampled, and purchased, enough wine to last us for the next two to three years.

Returning to Paris from Bordeaux, I reflected on the previous almost four years. I believe my DAO team and I fully succeeded in keeping the "punish France" policy from harming long-term relations between the French and US militaries, even during a period described by some as "the worst trans-Atlantic crisis in fifty years."

To be sure, there were many others who were prominent in minimizing the damage, with still others making things much better. After 1966, when France forced NATO to relocate its headquarters from Paris to Brussels and Mons, while still a member of the NATO Alliance, the French had operated entirely outside of NATO's integrated military command structure. Under General Jones's leadership, that began to quietly change in 2003.

From my perspective, I believe General Jim Jones's placing of fifteen French officers on NATO's integrated military staff during his first year of command was a significant success, if not a breakthrough. Within two to three years that number would grow to over 100 French military officers and soldiers, sailors, and airmen serving on NATO's integrated military staff for the first time since the mid-1960s. As is sometimes the case in events like these, General Jones deserved more credit than he got for bringing the French back into NATO's integrated military command structure and keeping overall relations from deteriorating to the point of dysfunction.

The same can also be said for General Henri Bentégeat. His taking the high ground after months of a "punish France" policy as well as partnership with General Jones no doubt aided (and was likely indispensable to) France's rejoining NATO's integrated command structure. By 2009, France would be fully back under the NATO tent, but the groundwork for this was laid by these two military leaders, Bentégeat and Jones. I believe the two US ambassadors, Howard Leach and Craig Stapleton, as well as a supporting cast of professional diplomats on the US Embassy Paris Country Team and US Mission to NATO, deserved some of the credit too.

Military attaché duty is not for everyone. It requires some aptitude, as well as just plain hard work, to learn a foreign language or two. It also demands a willingness to be open and to engage with other cultures while far from home, all on behalf of enhancing US-international relationships in the pursuit of US national and military interests, as well as those of our allies. One thing is for sure: while social events are part of the diplomatic landscape, attaché duty is not about cocktail parties and "holding your pinkie finger right," as some might like to claim.

For almost four years, I was honored to be called a "military attaché" in the service of my country. I was also privileged to serve with some extraordinary men and women. Among those were our indispensable US Foreign Service diplomats, who work tirelessly beyond the tweets and sound-bites to ensure that what was in the fine print was what America bargained for, and that America's interests were represented as well as they could be in peace and in war; indeed, in any international context and scenario.

Perhaps most importantly, I believe military attachés make a difference in strengthening international military *trust*, while conveying—at least in the American experience—American goodwill, and affecting how people beyond our borders and shores perceive Americans, and moreover, American military service women and men. At this moment somewhere in the world, from Argentina and Azerbaijan to Uzbekistan and Zimbabwe, a US military attaché, often with his or her family at their side, is doing just that.

IN MEMORIAM

Colonel (French Army, Ret) Charles "Charlie" Deleris; Sergeant First Class (US Army, Ret) Erik Math; and Mr. Joseph Phillip "Phil" Rivers, highly respected colleagues and fondly remembered fellow travelers with me on my French journey. May Almighty God eternally bless them.

ACKNOWLEDGMENTS

AS ANY FORTHRIGHT AUTHOR WILL declare, writing a book is a team sport. I was fortunate to have had many players on my all-star team who helped make this labor of love become a reality. I humbly and thankfully acknowledge their contributions:

My wife, Susan, who set the example for me by writing the first book in our family. Her scrapbooking hobby also resulted in a much unanticipated benefit many years later. Her assistance, guidance, and suggestions to the manuscript were also invaluable.

Author, friend, and extraordinary public servant Dennis Mansfield, for his encouragement to "write more," and for his personal example of writing excellence and insightful suggestions for improving the manuscript.

Major General (US Army, Ret) Gordon "Skip" Davis; Peter Lengyel, CEO; Tom Shanahan, national sportswriter; and my daughter Erika Nicole Steinke, for their exceptionally helpful reviews and recommendations for the manuscript.

My daughter Maria Nicole Steinke, for help with copies of the manuscript and suggestions for improving the photos and cover.

Melissa Gray, for her highly experienced and amazingly talented eye for copy-editing, and for significantly improving the original manuscript.

Paul Jacobsmeyer, Defense Office of Prepublication and Security Review, US Department of Defense, who received my manuscript as his first manuscript on his first day on the job, diligently guiding it through the clearance procedures required by no less than eight US government departments and agencies.

The entire team, including T. Campbell and Kellie Emery, at Koehler Books. Their exceptional competence, enthusiasm and professionalism made my first book publication not only fun, but enriching and rewarding.

James Patterson's Master Class. While the class was predominantly focused on writing fiction, Mr. Patterson's writing insights were invaluable and indeed masterful.

CPSIA information can be obtained
at www.ICGtesting.com
Printed in the USA
BVHW071223100222
628586BV00001B/98

9 781633 939448